landscape transformations

urbicus

green vision

landscape transformations

urbicus
jean-marc gaulier

DESIGN MEDIA PUBLISHING LIMITED

Open-air theatre in Mantes-la-Jolie, 2006.

foreword

As a medium between Man and nature, the landscape is a synthesis of human action on the environment. The landscape is the result of the perpetual process of Man's transformation of nature.

Sorry landscapes are born from the excessive pressure exerted on our land, from Man's predation on nature, from giving the economy prevalence over society. The landscape is a gauge of the quality of our projects for society. And all too often they fall short, with the "landscape arts" too often serving as an alibi.

Transforming our attitude to landscape is therefore necessary and indispensable for transforming what we want for society.

Sustainable development is the societal project that seeks to balance the social, the environmental and the economic. Landscape architecture is the result of these same equilibria applied to land areas. Sustainability is the very essence of landscape architecture.

The global and sustainable project is a means of transformation.

Whether it is natural, rural or urban, the landscape pre-exists. The landscape architect doesn't create landscapes, he reveals them, gives them back their value, sustains them or transforms them.

The landscape does not belong to us, it is the way the Land Area expresses itself, and this Land Area (or territoire in French) is a "common heritage of the Nation" (article L.110 of the French town planning code). Landscape projects are not our playing fields, but are the result of a shared project, of sites revealed, of fulfilling a social commission, and of responsible transformation.

Photo of the cover: The Blavet riverside fringes at Inzinzac-Lochrist (buildings: DDL Architectes).

We avoid approaching the project from the angle of narcissistic creativity, professional originality or media-friendly novelty. We insist on a project methodology that aims to produce coherent solutions to clearly identified problems through an attentive and inventive approach to the sites.

The sustainability of these answers depends on a certain economy of means, a modesty vis-à-vis the site and its inhabitants, taking natural phenomena into account, putting in place ordinary strategies and rejecting an excess of personal expression.

A landscape project means a site revealed and informed by drawing up a programme, putting challenges in order of priority, distinct action scenarios, listening to partners and working together.

The quality of a project therefore comes from asking pertinent questions, finding coherent solutions, and the sustainability of a transformation process.

Landscape architecture means a sustainable form of town planning where the landscape is liveable, a viable quality of living, an urban and natural landscape that makes the most of its assets, a land area development that is economical and balanced.

We dream of seeing land area development methods transformed, so that the landscape would not result from the individual and non-consultative impulse of the farmer, the ecologist, the architect or town planner, the engineer and the contractor and their respective ministries, but be protected by an administrative body whose vocation would be to produce an overall development of the land area through a sustainable landscape.

We strive for the landscape no longer to be a no-comment juxtaposition of landscapes protected as historical or natural heritage, landscapes sacrificed for the benefit of economic activity and forgotten landscapes, overgrown or "useless", but instead a coherent shared project where the landscape reflects a balanced society.

The invention of new landscapes has to involve the inventory of the old ones. Only through a critical study of the existing landscapes, considering the economic, environmental and social practices of the past, can we produce sustainable landscapes for the 21st century.

With this plurigraphic collection – neither a monograph nor a biography – we simply wish to testify to the multitude of methods of acting, and to review chosen projects to illustrate that the landscape is a pertinent way of considering the problems of land area development.

This book shows the work of a team that wishes to demonstrate the diversity of landscape architects' practices, not for themself, but to show the value of landscape architecture. This disciplinary field is not sufficiently recognised as such in 21st-century France, but could be a unifying force for our societal projects. The practice of architect-landscape architect, or of landscape "gardener", should be recognised etymologically, as "civic builder" is in architecture.

Open-air theatre in Mantes-la-Jolie, view of the abbey, 2006.

contents

architecture of the land — 010

sharing space and the shared city — 012

a project as a whole, a project together — 056

the "naturbanity" — 076

a "positive city" — 078

a new economy of landscape — 110

projects index — 130

biography-agency — 132

contributions — 133

credits — 134

architecture of the land

The landscape is a living architecture, a superimposition of human history and natural history, of environmental stratifications and social practices whose project is in perpetual motion. It is a volume in a cavity, the moulding of nature by our society, a tangible organisation of the impalpable environment, the architecture of boundaries that transforms the invisible cadastre into visible plots, the infinite mosaic resulting from our practices, and the juxtaposition of several uncoordinated projects.

The landscape, as a collection of things seen, has an aesthetic and tangible dimension, but we want to objectify it as a social project and to approach it as a way of architecting uses, ecology and economy. The landscape is an "architecture of the land".

The landscape composes our identities. As representative of our societies, it is our social identity. As our personal address, it defines others' view of ourselves and the image we send back to them.

Mistreating the landscape is a way of disfiguring ourselves, of devaluing our identity, scorning history, mutilating our roots and unbalancing natural environments. A debased landscape cannot be lived in. Industrialised agriculture is a one-sided rural economy and an accident waiting to happen. An anonymous housing estate is a ghetto where an absence of landscape to enhance the living environment is synonymous with social death.

Landscape structures the uses of a land area, the space in which we conduct our relationships with others, the reach of our means of transport, the quality of our food and the consequences of our economic practices on the environment.

As landscape architects, we are the builders of this architecture, which is the only kind that integrates the understanding of uses, time and natural phenomena.

Fountain garden for the Vallet mediatheque
(Building: David Cras Architecte).

Sharing space and the shared city

Public space is an urban facility that organises and defines the city. The consumerist city, juxtaposing and piling up functionalities, pollutes and impoverishes the land area. In the grip of its fascination with the motor car, the 20th-century based the dimensions of its cities on the width of vehicles.

We must now take a new view of the place of the car in cities by "de-vehicling" both the space and our preconceptions. From an economic point of view, we cannot envisage getting rid of cars completely, but the shared car, pooled parking spaces, the replacement of the car on short journeys by soft transport, the improvement of public transport and clean cars are among the hypotheses that will cause a revolution in the urban landscape.

The electric car will make it possible for the borders of motorways, which cannot be lived on today, to become urban. If speed is not an issue, the road can become a street, a place where cars and pedestrians cohabit. If the possession of a car is not a sign of social status, car pooling and a reduction in the number of parking spaces will generate room for other uses.

Through its siuation, its proportions, its essence, outside space places and exhibits the constructions in the city. The boundaries, the fences, define the transition between public and private space. The vocabulary of this space must complement that of the architecture. The stratification of the vegetation creates an intermediate height between the building and the pedestrian.

Landscape, the architecture of a land area, is mainly concerned with expressing the limits and the new necessities of a mixed and balanced sharing of the space.

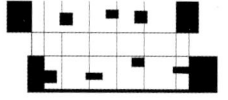 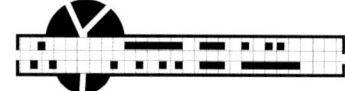 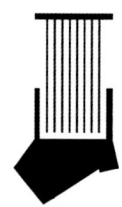 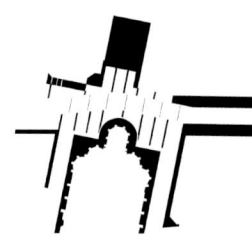

Feltre and Calvaire streets

Situated in a protected historic sector, Feltre and Calvaire streets form the busiest shopping area in the centre of Nantes.

The project has transformed two ordinary streets into a pedestrian zone crossed by more than 300 buses a day. The disappearance of cars, and the organisation of the bus interchange and deliveries, have provided space for pedestrians and trees in a wide, urban courtyard.

The links with the neighbouring streets and the squares have been reworked. In particular the apse of Saint Nicolas's church has been transformed into a series of low-rising, wide steps to facilitate the path of pedestrians.

Blocks of yellow granite house the urban amenities linked to public transport and the shops. Giant bamboo plants and stand-alone sweetgum trees create an attractive urban atmosphere that has raised the image of the street in the minds of Nantes's inhabitants.

Opposite page: The street axis and the pocket gardens created on the small squares.
Above: The street during the construction work and after it was completed.

Opposite page: Details of the granite and the asphalte, economical materials.
Above: The small squares and the granite blocks.

Opposite page: The paving is all in granite slabs and asphalte.
Above: The nighttime atmosphere in the street.

Europe avenue

La Grande Motte was created in the 1960s by the architect Jean Balladur. Now listed as French architectural heritage, the town aims to continue its urban development in the spirit of the original plan. Designed as a summer beach resort, it became a permanently inhabited town where the sharing of the space and architectural quality are the driving forces for renewal.

The avenue has been transformed into a long plateau that crosses town, ending in the sea. Evolving through the seasons, it brings into play three small squares that can be adapted to different uses. A graphic charter harmonises the terraces and businesses along the avenue, where the urban furniture has been specially redesigned.

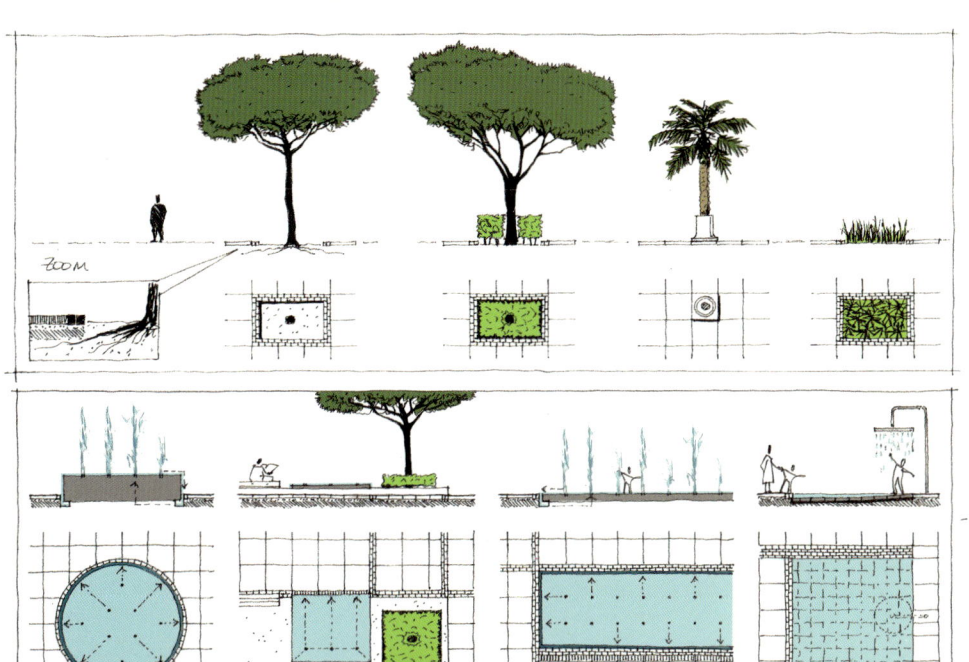

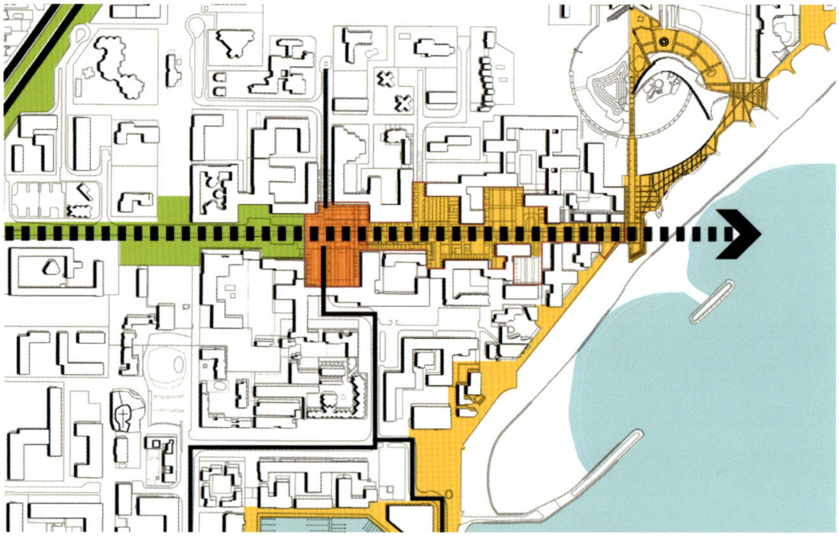

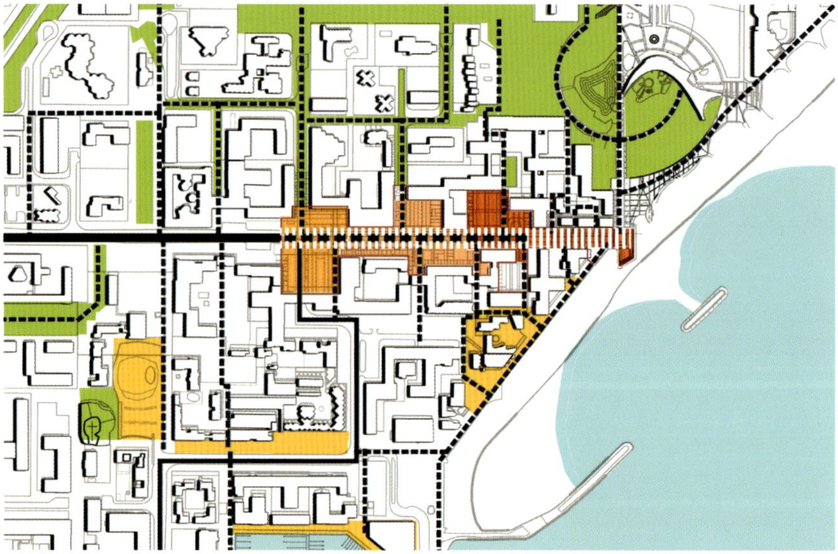

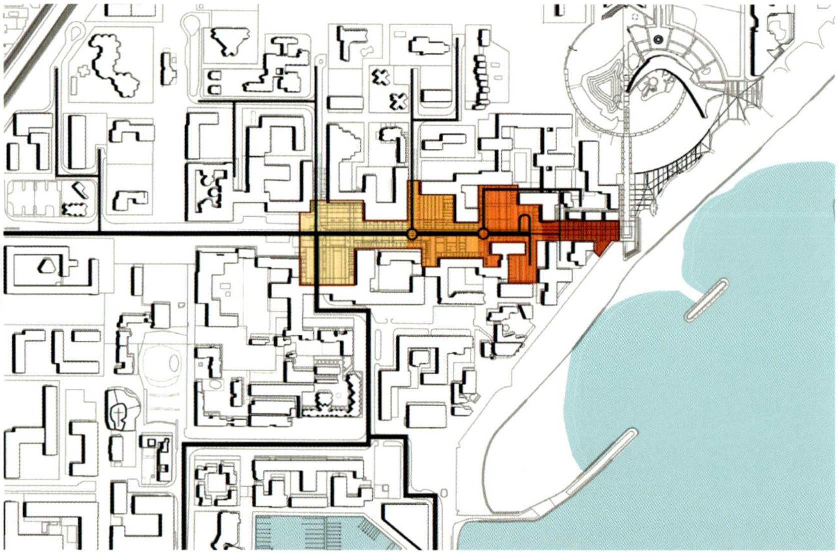

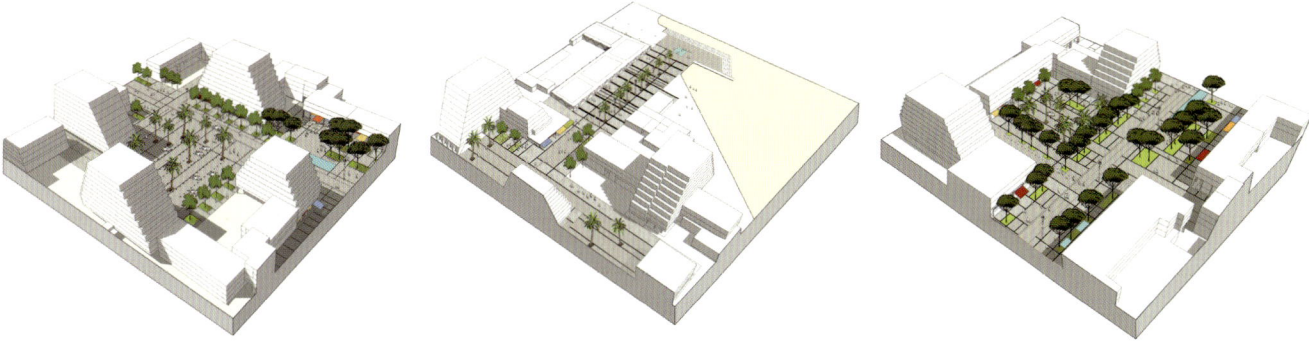

Opposite page: The project strategies.
Above: A street transformed into a shared esplanade.

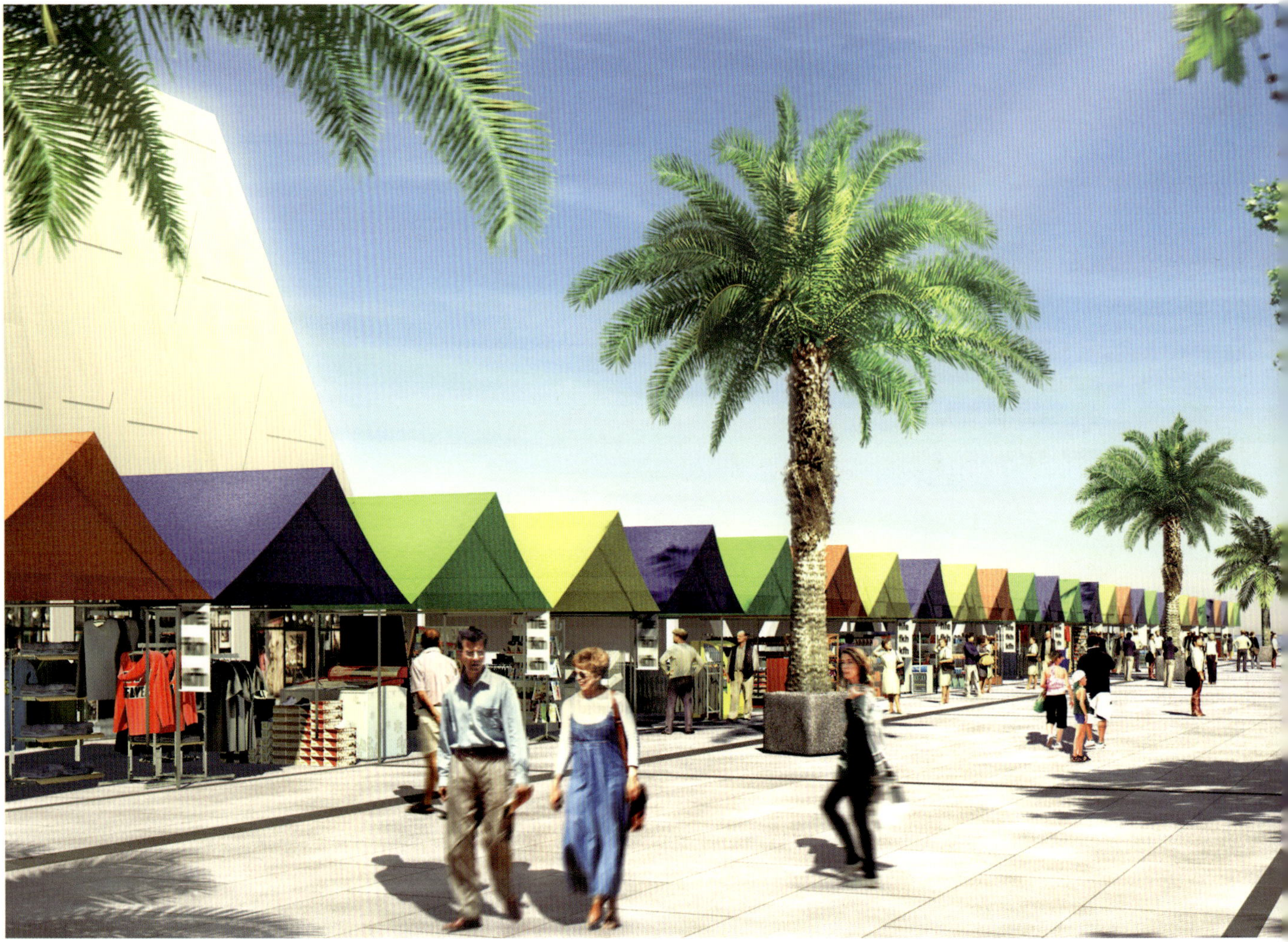

CARTHAGE MILK
Artima
BIJOUX - CADEAUX

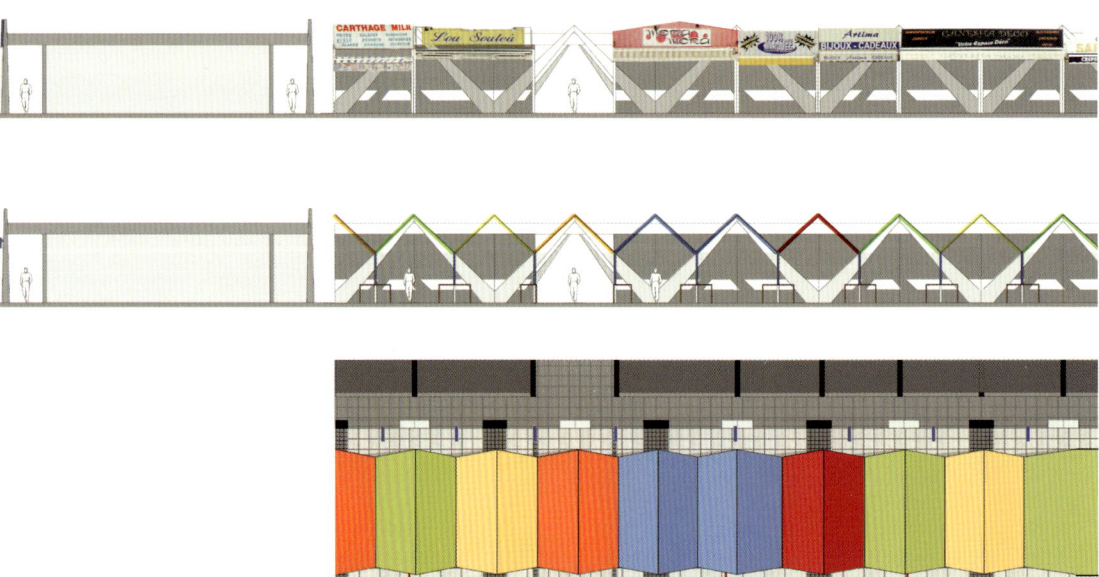

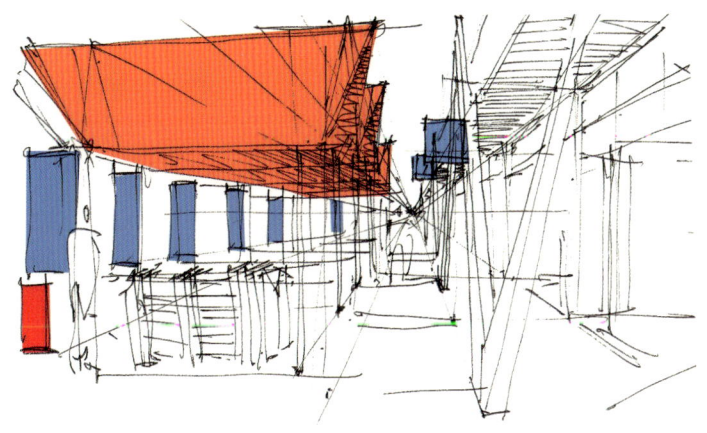
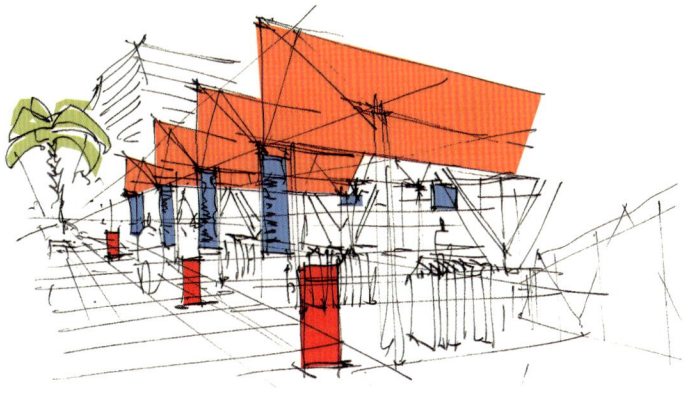

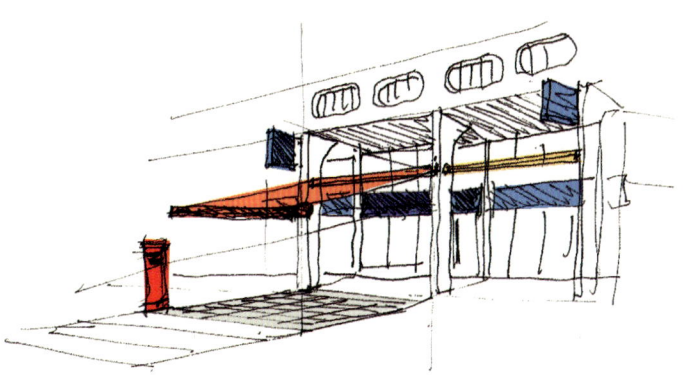

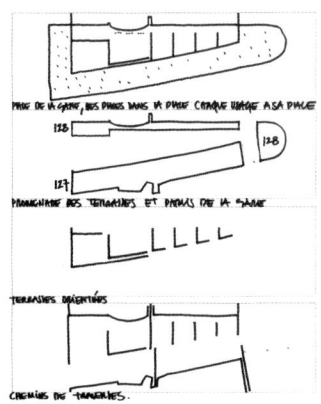 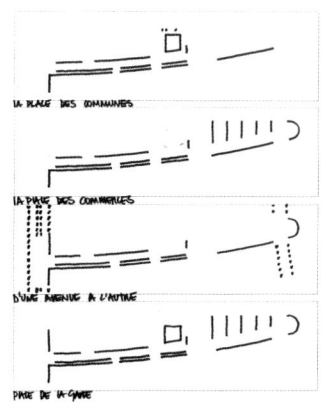 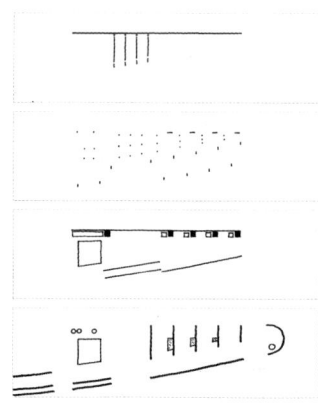

Ariane square

The speed of urbanisation in new towns is such that you sometimes have to imagine a square before the town itself even exists. Located in Marne-la-Vallée, and forming a continuation of the Val d'Europe shopping centre and its RER (high-speed suburban rail) station, Ariane square forms a gateway to the infrastructure of Disneyland Paris for the many tourists who visit.

Beyond this, the square has to fulfil its role as a structuring public space for the town centre. It brings together several uses (RER station, shopping centre, restaurant terraces, the town's music school, offices…).

It is planned around three space typologies:
- an esplanade planted with rows of trees that frame the views towards the restaurant terraces,
- a forecourt forming the link between the RER station entrance and an unusual building in the urban facade,
- a pavement garden (built over an underground carpark) slightly below the forecourt, which offers a quiet space accessible to the nearby residential neighbourhood.

The levelling is a subtle structuring element of the square. The use of pollarded linden trees as a curtain is inspired by the traditional vocabulary of the local square but, planted in an unusual way, they create a transition between history and modernity.

ROMA

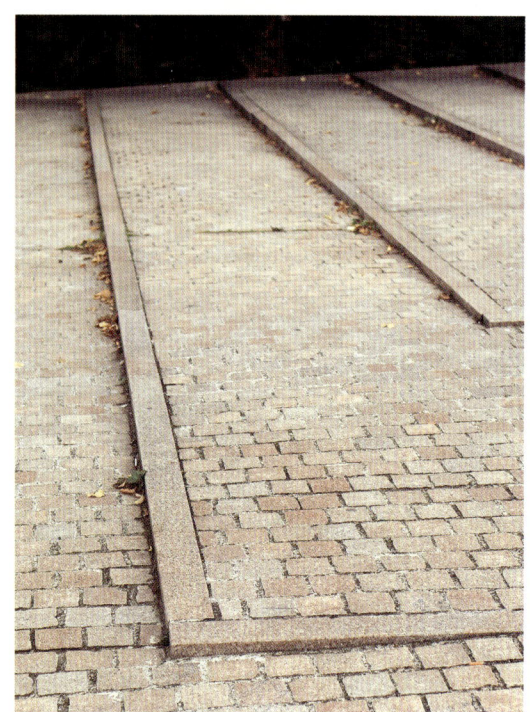

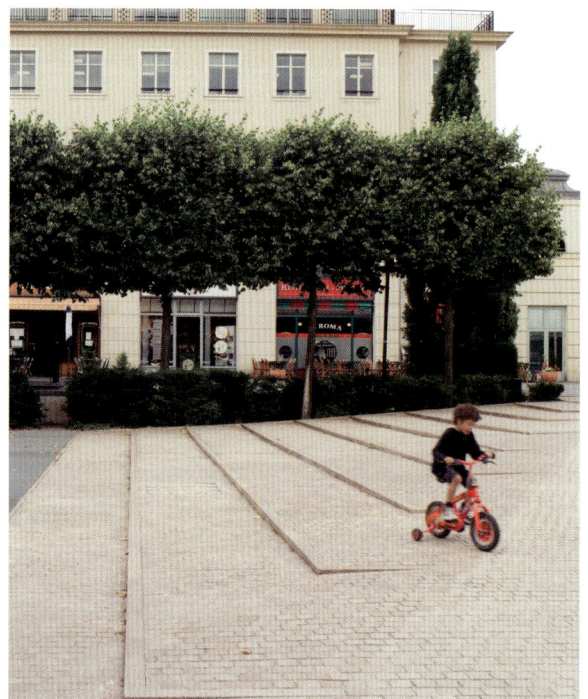

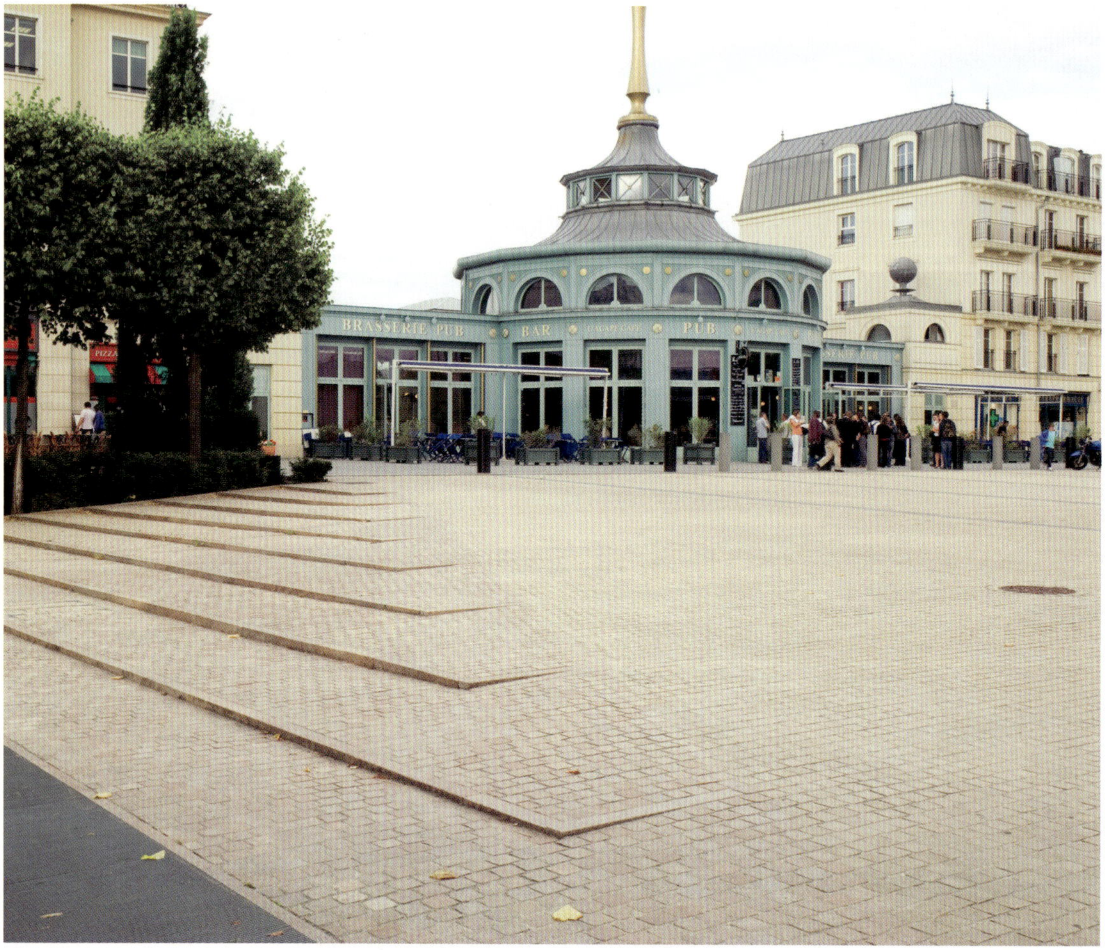
BRASSERIE PUB
BAR
PUB
PIZZA

Lochrist town centre

On the banks of the Blavet, around 20 km north-east of Lorient, the commune of Inzinzac-Lochrist (population 5,800) has historically been organised around three settlements with distinct urban functions:
- Penquesten, an autonomous rural village separated from the rest of the conurbation by Tremelin forest
- Inzinzac, surrounded by agricultural land, where the Town Hall is situated
- Lochrist, a workers' town that developed from 1860 with the arrival on the banks of the Blavet of the Hennebont ironworks (the mainstay of the Breton iron and steel industry); the main shops and services are gathered here.

The closure of the ironworks at the end of the 1960s left a large brownfield site, but above all an exceptional riverside site with its system of island, dam and quays.

The regeneration of Lochrist's public spaces forms the framework for a project across the commune that aims to:
- intensify the town centre by developing Lochrist in a way that strengthens it as the heart of the conurbation,
- identify Lochrist within the greater Lorient area as "rurban" and "naturban" – between town and countryside,
- perpetuate and develop the shopping facilities,
- develop mixed and diversified housing,
- encourage soft modes of transport,
- improve safety by putting in place an anti-flood scheme for the Blavet.

After almost 10 years' work under the exceptional impetus of the local authority, the project, ambitious for a settlement of this size, has allowed us to transform the image of the town while making the most of its unique history.

The public spaces have been strengthened by:
- the creation of a riverside path and a footbridge over the quays,
- the improvement of different squares in the context of a network, and the organisation of parking,
- the creation of riverbank- or dock- gardens on the Blavet, and the uncovering of a stream,
- the improvement of the main artery through the town centre.

Opposite page: The foundry at the height of production, and the Blavet shore after the regeneration work.
Above: The public spaces of the town centre, evoking the lines of the old foundry.

The public "dock-gardens" link the town to the walk laid out on the old industrial quay. (Buildings: DDL Architectes)

François Mitterrand square acts as a hinge for the different ground levels and connecting roads.

34

Opposite page: Blavet garden and J. Legrand island.
Above: Foundry square and the Blavet quay laid out with an industrial vocabulary. (Rehabilitated building: David Cras Architecte)

Austerlitz quay

The wide and built-up Austerlitz quayside, which, with other Parisian quays enjoys UNESCO World Heritage status, has an unusual form and poses an unusual challenge in the urban project of eastern Paris.

With the traffic circulation removed, it was possible to plan a programme that unites the activities of the city and the port, extends the riverside walk and creates a new relationship between the neighbourhoods beside it and the Seine.

The quay is laid out as a broad esplanade paved in sandstone, forming a garden of interstices where the planted spaces between the paving stones are, in their own small way, conducive to biodiversity. The levelling makes it accessible to all without hindering the flow of the Seine at high water, and the paving materials have been chosen to prioritise the way the city will use the space.

Above: The quays of the Seine, or how to reappropriate Paris's largest public spaces.
Opposite page: From a brownfield formerly used as roads to the project in progress.

Gironde quays

Internationally renowned for its great wines, Pauillac is also a town hard-hit by the disappearance of its industry.

Pauillac's quays, 1.2 km long, are the main public space of the commune. Their nobility comes from their wide landscapes looking out to the geography beyond. They form the basis for a project for improving the town and giving it back its dignity.

From the limestone facades to the shores of the Gironde, several walks succeed each other through built or natural environments. As a continuation of Lafayette esplanade, on the main axis from the town centre, a garden irrigated by the estuary offers a new convivial space.

The broad stretches of protected natural shoreline guided the project towards a plan that makes the most of the estuary landscapes and the relationship with the water.

Three walks run longitudinally from the facades up to the shore:
- the "Terraces" walk reconfigures the pavement in front of the shops and offers a garden running along the front of the residential buildings, enhancing the local architecture;
- the "Great Trees" walk weaves a setting around the plane trees and integrates the parking;
- the "Estuary" walk runs along the existing protective wall, which has been widened, and onto a pontoon from which you can watch the reedbed and the river.

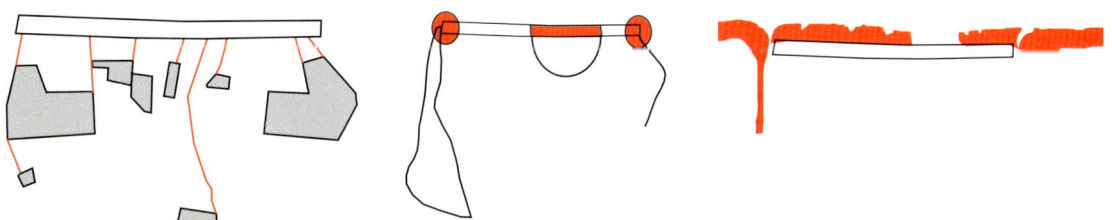

The three walks: the terraces, the avenue of trees, and the Gironde.

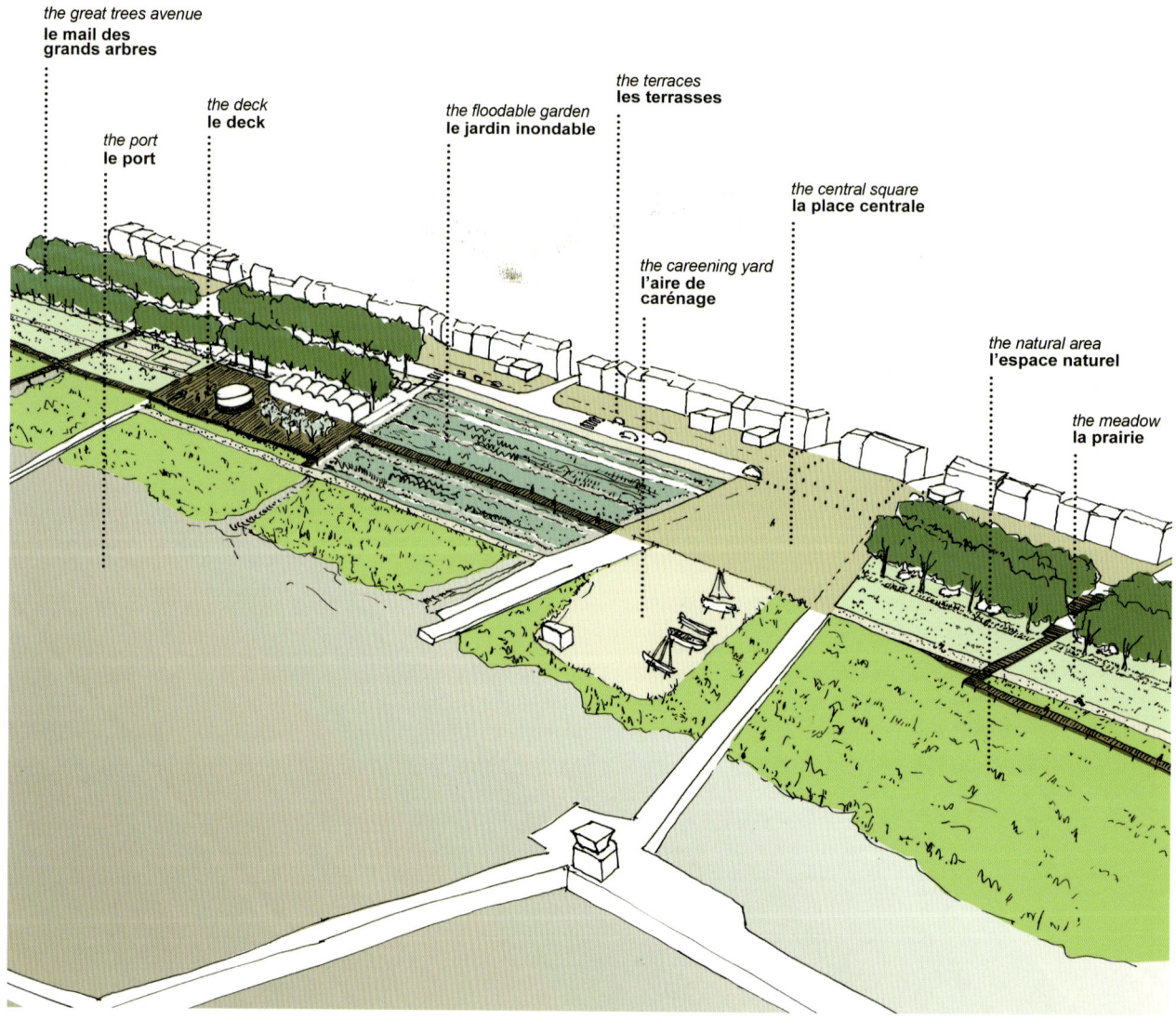

Above: The garden irrigated by the Gironde and its links to the quays.
Opposite page: From busy road to promenade, the reinvestment of public space.

Opposite page: The landscaped Gironde walk; the furniture is made using traditional cooperage skills.
Above: From the existing dockland terrain to a floodable garden.

Beler gateway

This site, which straddles the two French departments of Moselle and Meurthe-et-Moselle and faces the ambitious Belval project (20,000 jobs and 5,000 homes), forms part of the development strategy for an eco-conurbation on the France-Luxembourg border.

Organised around rural landscapes dedicated to leisure activities and nearby organic agriculture, these attractive French land reserves offered an opportunity to create affordable housing for Luxembourg, cross-border amenities and opportunities for trade. Transforming a road into a residential boulevard, and drawing on a shared history to form a cross-border population pool, landscape architecture is here an economic, social and environmental project.

The project is built around the Beler valley, the source of Luxembourg's main river, the Alzette. Thinking beyond borders, the approach is guided by the theme of sustainable development, the complementary nature of the two countries' planning strategies, environmental continuity, shared policies on border-crossing, and development strategies that make the most of the strengths and weaknesses of both states' economies.

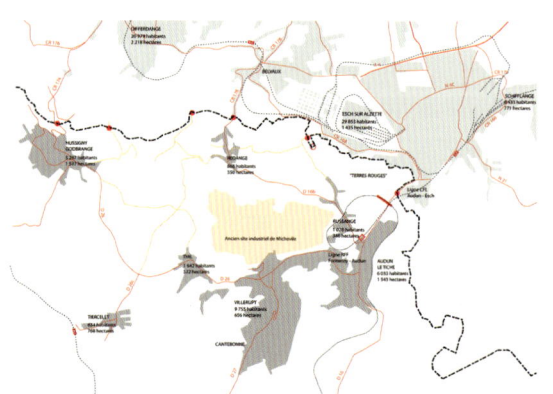
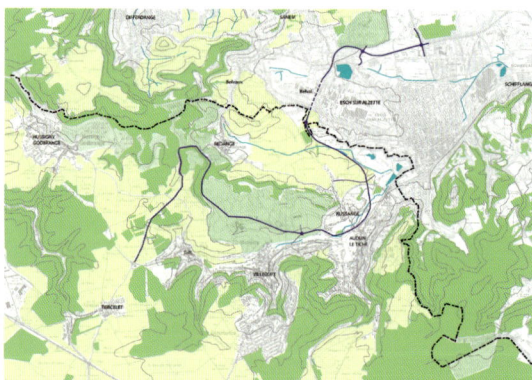

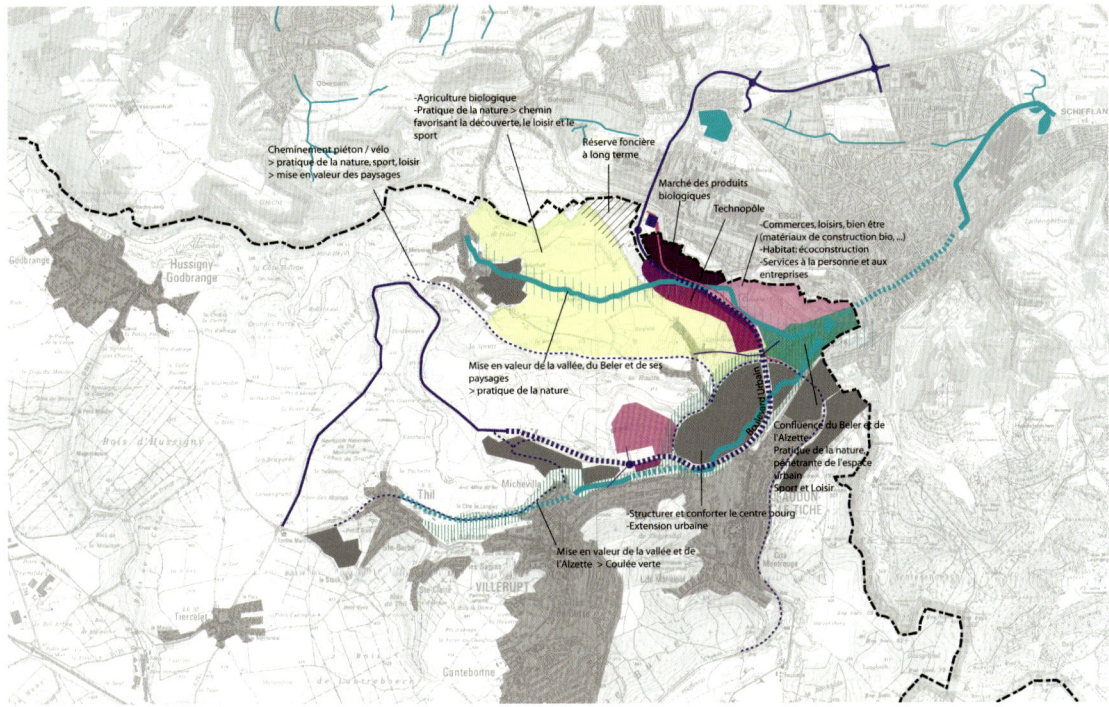

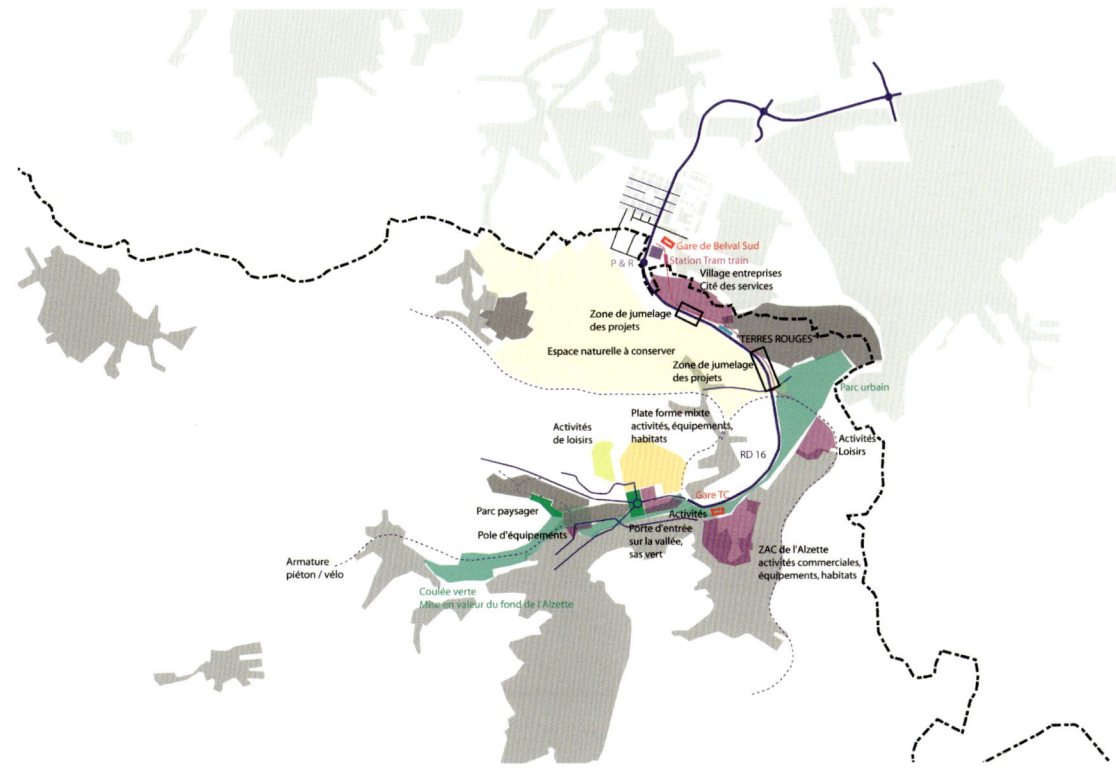

Opposite page: Before work began: the road, urban and landscape networks of a cross-border territory.
Above: Planning map and synthesis of the projects in progress for a coordinated land development scheme.

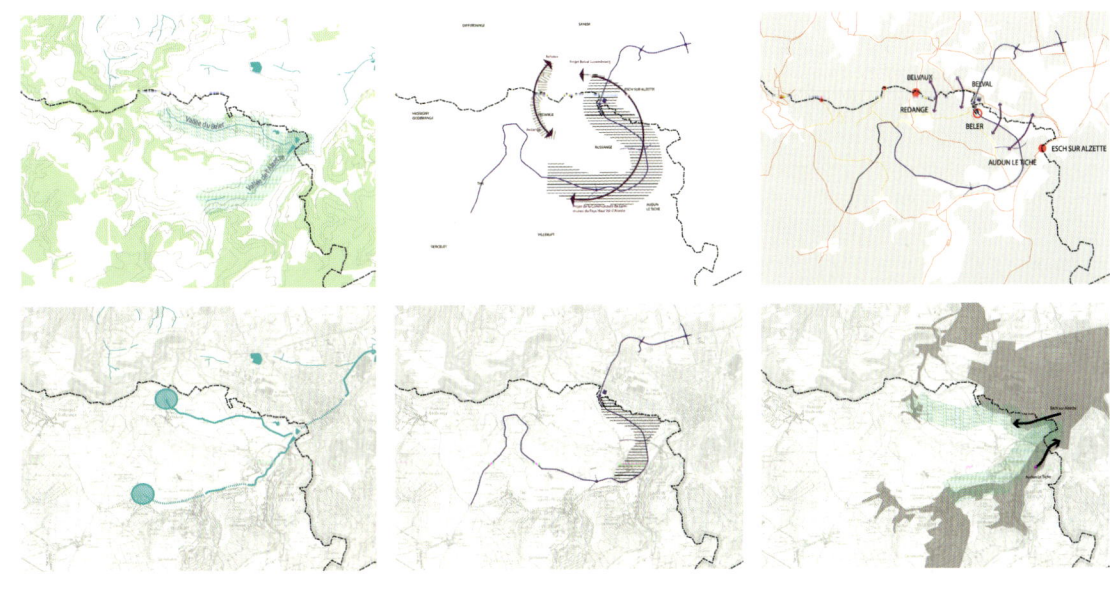

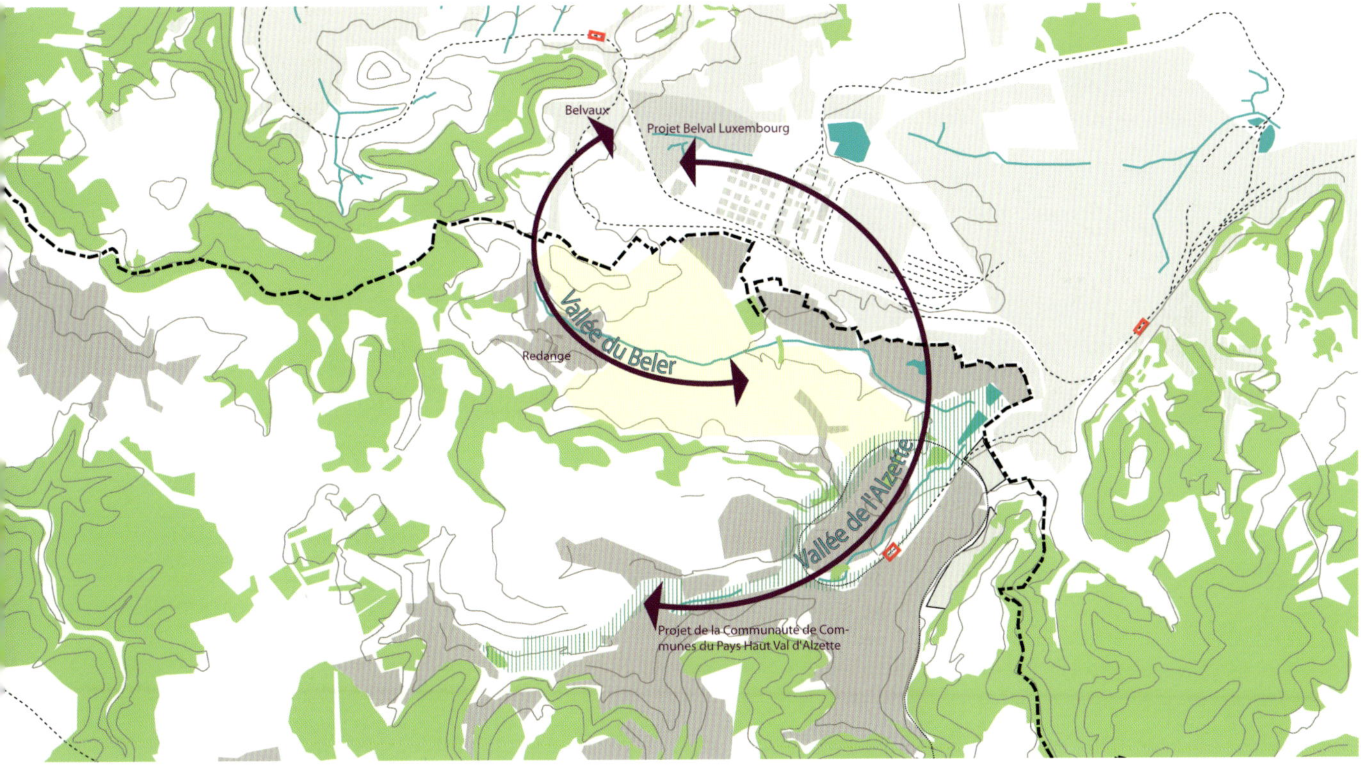

Opposite page: Before work began: the Alzette and Beler valley, a cross-border landscape, and the Belval gateway (Luxembourg). Above: A reading of the space and the strengths of the territory, designed to encourage complementary planning.

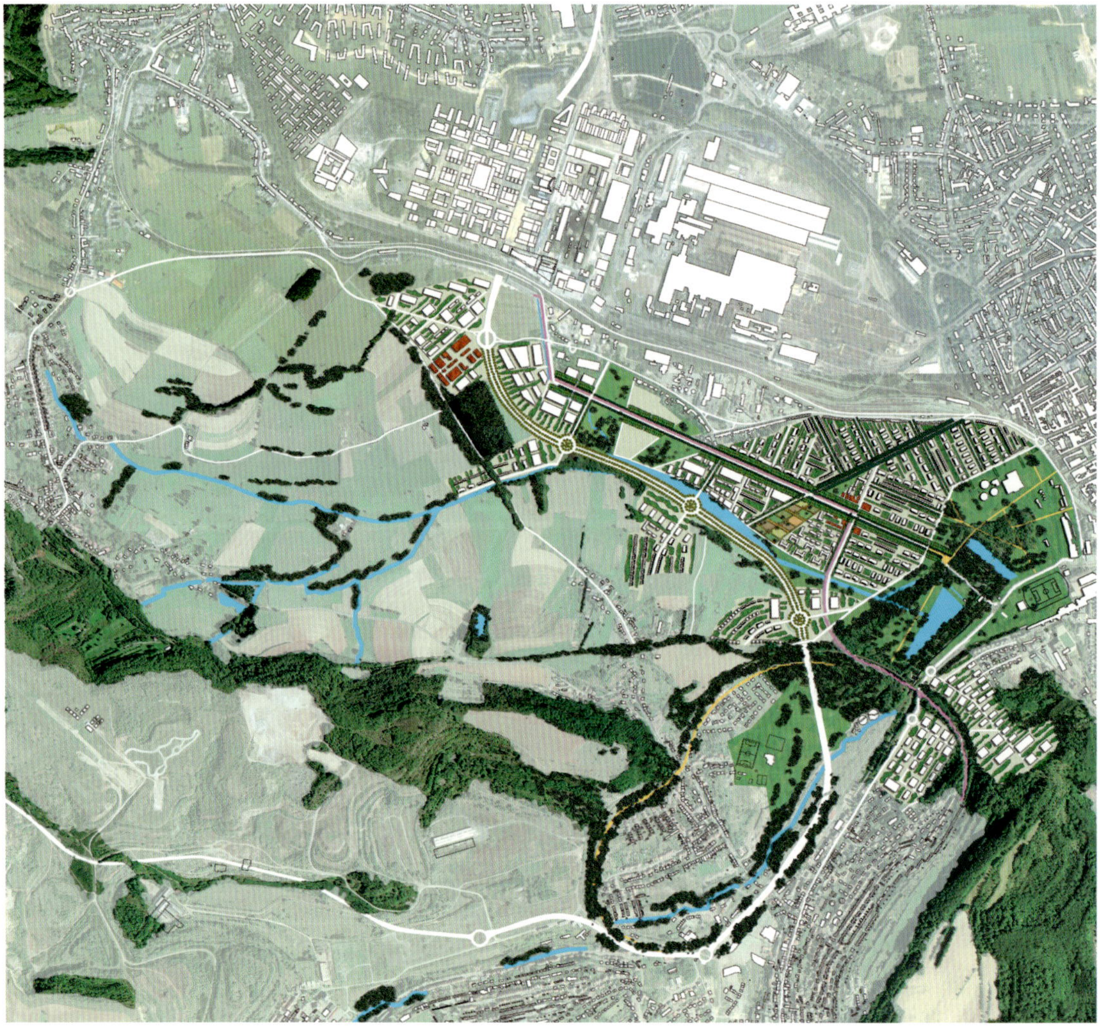

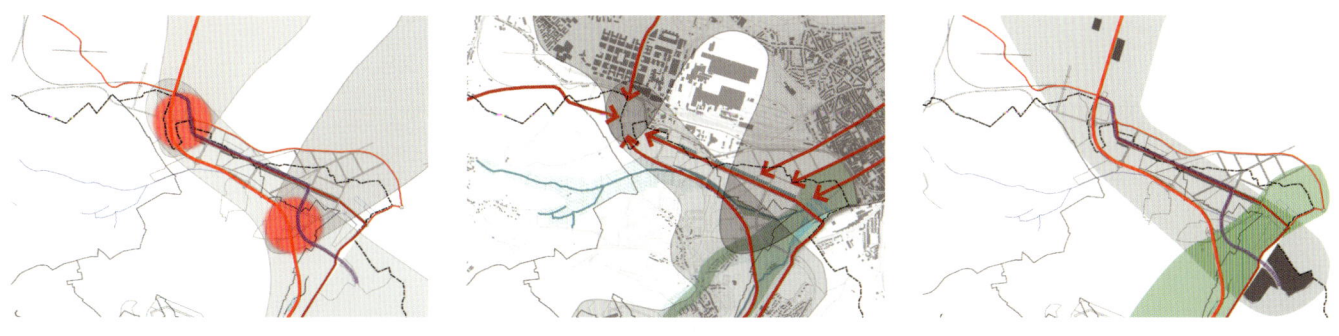

Opposite page and this page, top: The development of the territory by theme, showing its urban, economic, landscape and environmental impacts.
Above: Perspective ground plan of the project.

Saint-Charles pit

Located on the German border in a mining and ironworking region, Petite Rosselle is looking for a new lease of life after the demise of its industry.

The town was shaped by the mining that went on here from the end of the 19th century: its topography has been uprooted by the mining infrastructure, the concentrations of workers' housing reveal the chronology of the successive pit openings, the paths retrace the workers' routes, and the "natural" spaces are the neglected areas that could not be exploited as mines. The history of the town and its urban form are indissociable and interlinked with that of the mine.

Today the commune is in limbo, from a spatial as well as a social point of view: the housing is run-down, shops are closing, there is a lack of services and the town centre is hardly recognisable as such.

The guide plan that has been developed gives coherence to this fragmented territory while revitalising it through cross-border dynamism and industrial tourism.

The urban project for the new town is based on the lines of the former mine. The mine headframe will become a reference point around which the centre and the mining estates revolve; the cultural centre will be in the former stables; a street that opens up the neighbourhoods is placed on the main axis of the factory; the railway lines become a cycle path; the settling ponds and the surrounding forest will be developed into a natural urban park.

Cassini map 1750

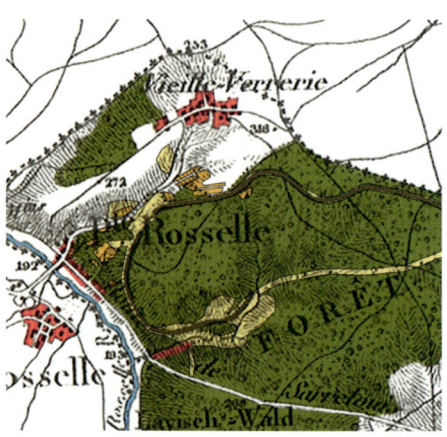

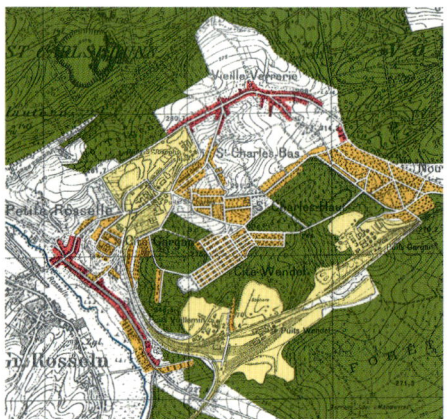

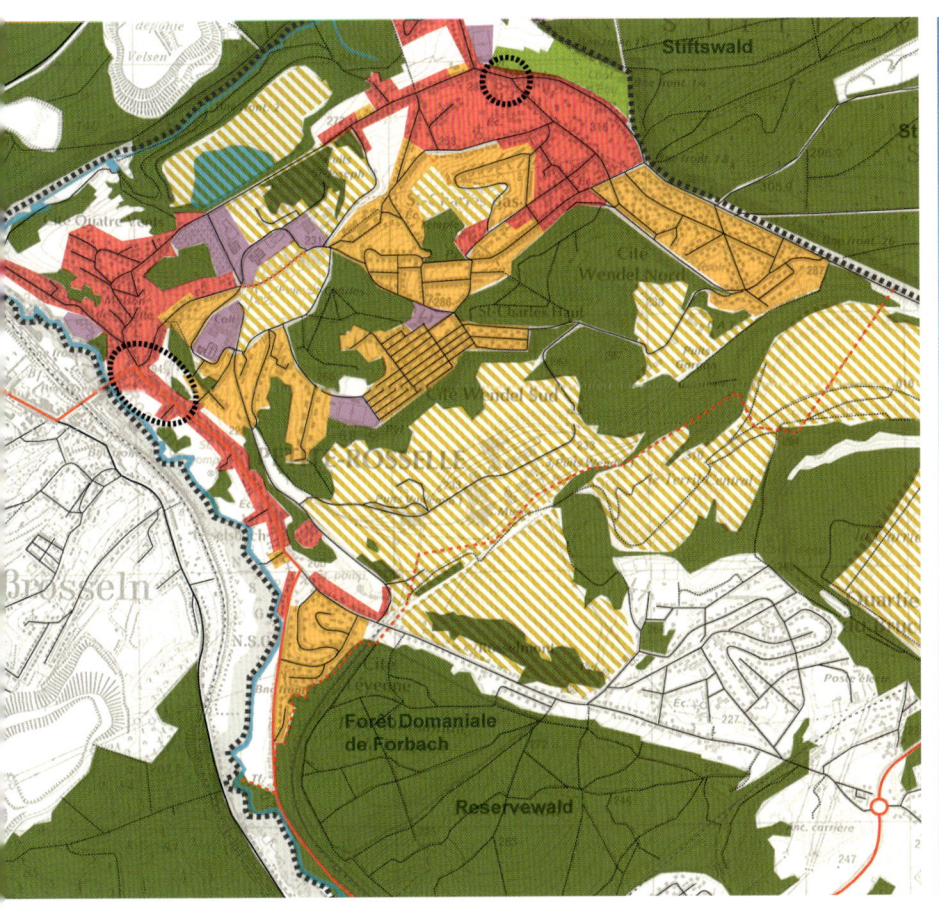

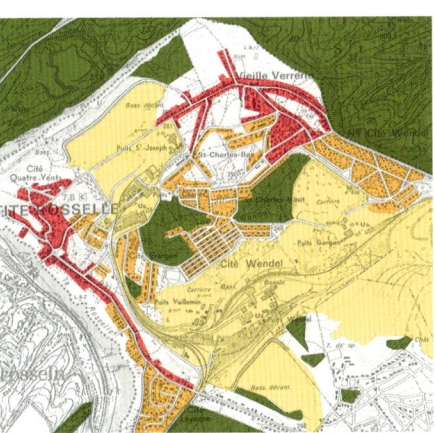
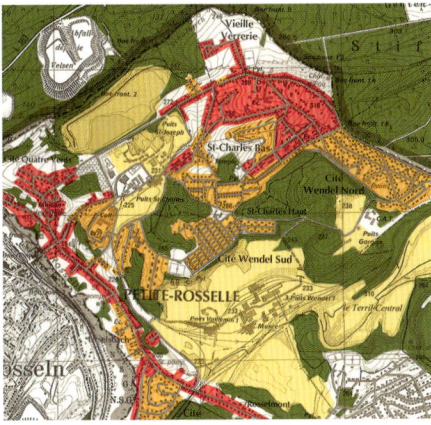

- the sports park
- shops and public facilities landscape
- new housing

Above: Organisational principles of the new neighbourhood.
Opposite page: After the factory town, the town replaces the factory.

The factory at the centre of the town has been replaced by a new neighbourhood organised around sports and cultural activities. The new housing is inspired by the form and density of the workers' estates.

The new neighbourhood will become the centre of the Cross-Border Conurbation Natural Park, a tourist centre linked to the museums of Carreau Wendel Mine, the largest mining site in France, and the Völklingenest factory, a German steelworks that has remained intact. With 140 new homes on the horizon in 2020, this site is regenerating thanks to his history and its landscape.

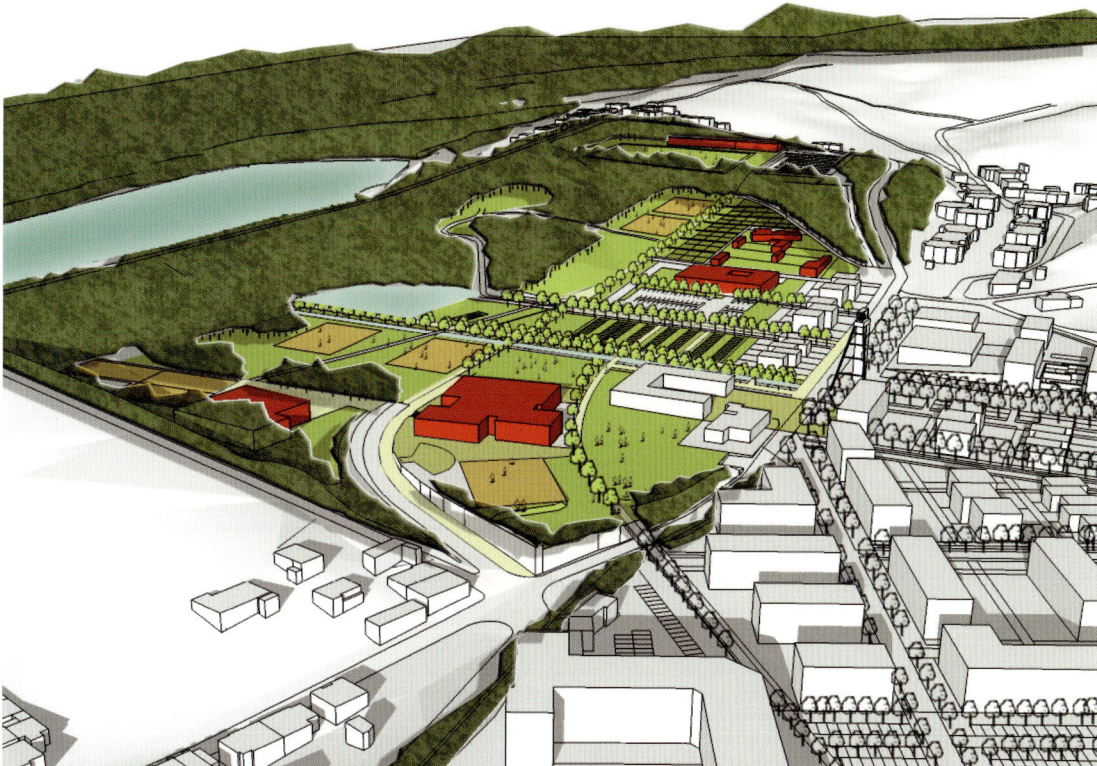

The Cormorans neighbourhood in Vandœuvre.

a project as a whole, a project together

Around our homes we park our cars, we manage our refuse, we play, we garden, we walk, we meet each other, we give an image to "our house", we make ourselves safe and we mark out the limits of our living space. Outside space has the potential for improving urban practices. What place is given to biodiversity, to the alternative management of water, to soft means of transport, to the well-considered management of our refuse, to pooled parking, to controlling noise and heat pollution, to light and shade, to community gardens and neighbourhood get-togethers? Often neglected, at best decorative, outside space is all too often forgotten in urban and architectural production. We must invest in it once again with a project based on use.

The use of the city is in constant evolution; new eco-citizen practices are emerging, and the space is used differently according to the weather and social origins. But how can we think sustainably about the city of tomorrow if these evolutions are not the departure point for our thinking on the architecture of the outdoors? How can town-planning experts be heard if the expertise of daily life is not recognised?

We are in favour of bringing in a means of measuring and studying usage that would refine the understanding and the demands of each social landscape. The consultation with and participation of the inhabitants are both means of enriching the programme, of bringing solutions adapted to different populations, of improving the conditions that will lead people to accept the changes linked to any project.

We only act on one part of the project, that of its design and implementation. The work of setting up the programme, the pertinent expression of the commission, the participation of the inhabitants and a consistent political will are also indispensable contributions to the success of a shared project. Any project that is whole must be done together.

Vandœuvre town centre

Vandœuvre-lès-Nancy (population 31,000), the second largest town in the Meurthe-et-Moselle department, was a rural Lorraine village that became a Priority Development Zone (Zone d'Urbanisation Prioritaire – ZUP) in the 1960s, when its towers and horizontal blocks were interwoven with the road infrastructure.

After this initial development, the town has gone into decline since the 1990s from a downslide in its demographic caused by the unsuitability of its housing, the obsolescence of its public spaces and the increasing poverty and ageing of its population.

Urbicus has been working on an urban restructuring project in the town of Vandœuvre since 1998.

The site before work began.

This urban renewal project concerns three neighbourhoods as well as the area around the Town Hall and the Nations centre. It is at the heart of a deprived urban area covering 160 hectares.

The Nations is both Vandœuvre's ailing shopping centre and its town centre. This central point, which is cut off by Boulevard de l'Europe (30,000 vehicle a day), is the focus of a redevelopment project that aims to make Vandœuvre an attractive shopping centre again.

Overall plan of the sectors studied.

The Kehl bridge, which cuts the town in two, will eventually be demolished, opening up new possibilities for urban housing.

Trèves-Fribourg and Forêt-Noire neighbourhoods will be restructured to modify their peripheries, open up new uses, rebuild diversified housing and reforge the urban identity. The Cormorans neighbourhood is essentially made up of a horizontal housing block 200 metres long that has been split up to open up the neighbourhood onto the redeveloped Town Hall square.

This restructuring work draws on the attractive landscapes of the Vandœuvre hillsides to enhance and strengthen its identity as a garden city.

Opposite page and above: The project before and after. Plants as the vocabulary of the urban restructuring.

The Cormorans neighbourhood after its completion in 2004.

Vitry suburbs

Vitry-le-François (population 15,000), the fourth largest town in the Marne department, was fortified by Francis I in the 16th century. It is situated at a crossroads of canals, railways and roads that encouraged its initial development but are now insufficient to ensure its future. Its neighbourhoods of public housing, based on large blocks, are impoverished, isolated, obsolete and run down.

The project aims to rehabilitate these areas, connect the neighbourhoods to the town centre and the station, open them up to the riverbanks and build new housing. The sense of disconnection caused by the mass of railways lines is reduced by the creation of a public garden and the rehabilitation of the station square, forming part of a network of public spaces across the town.

After a definition study submitted in 2005, the town decided to commit to 12 years of work with unwavering determination, in order to weave new links between the town centre and the suburbs.

Place Giraud
Projet en cours
Livraison fin 2012
Giraud square
Project in progress
Due for completion end 2012

Quartier Fauvarge
Concours 2004
Étude préliminaire 2006
Fauvarge neighbourhood
Competition 2004
Preliminary study 2006

Avenue Moll
Projet réalisé septembre 2009
Moll avenue
Project completion September 2009

Gare SNCF
Projet réalisé avril 2008
SNCF railway station
Project competition April 2008

Parc
Projet en cours
Livraison juin 2012
Park
Project in progress
Due for completion june 2012

Quartier Rome Saint-Charles
- Avenue Marcel Bailly
Projet en cours
Livraison fin 2012
- Quartier Résidentialisation
Projet en cours
Livraison fin 2016
Rome Saint-Charles neighbourhood
- Marcel Bailly avenue
Project in progress
Due for completion end 2012
- Residentialisation neighbourhood
Project in progress
Due for completion end 2016

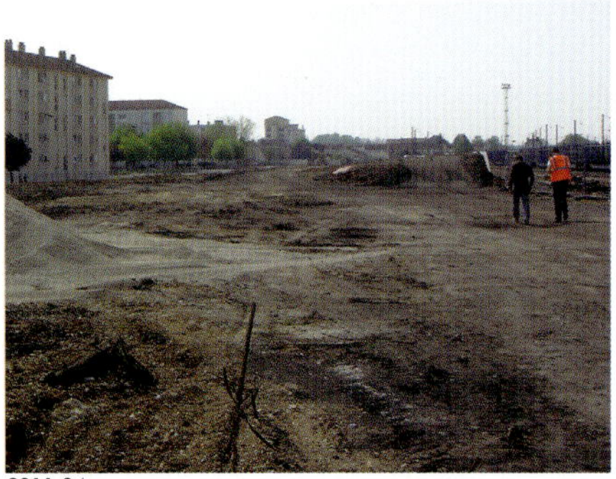
2011-04

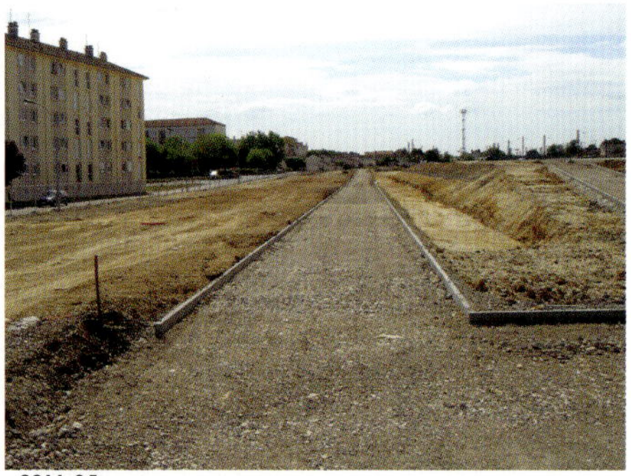
2011-05

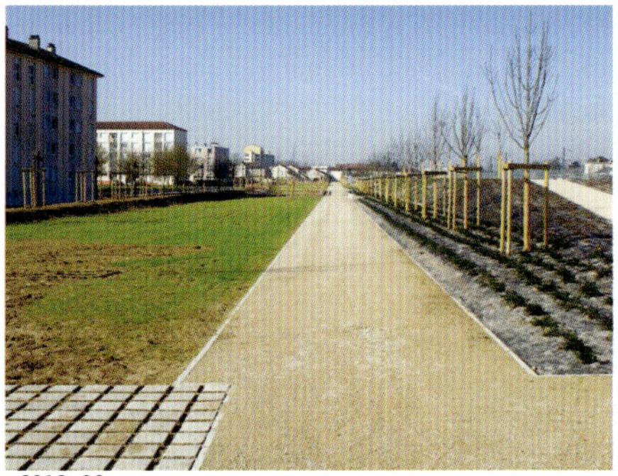
2012 -03

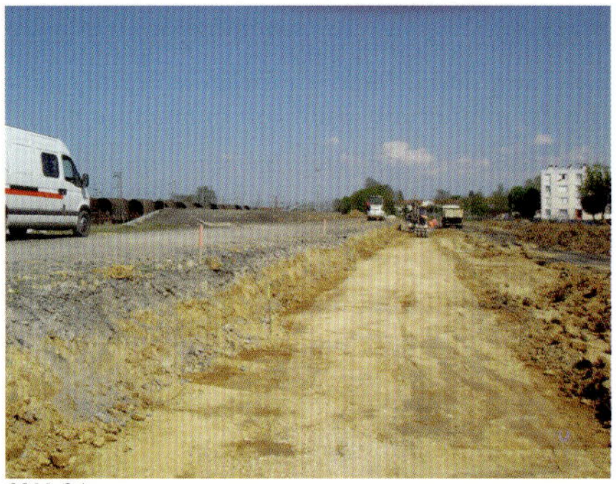
2011-04

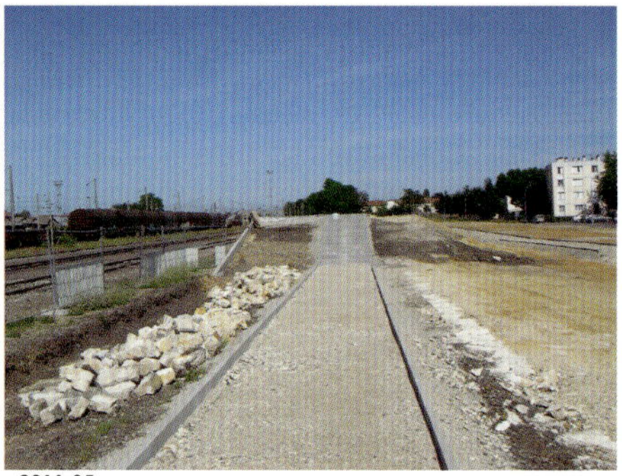
2011-05

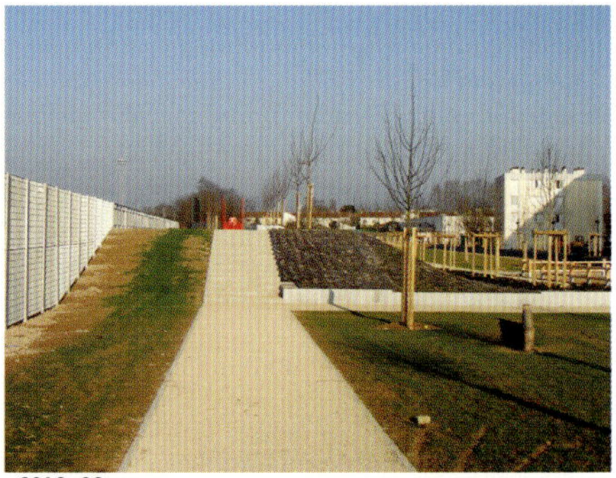
2012 -03

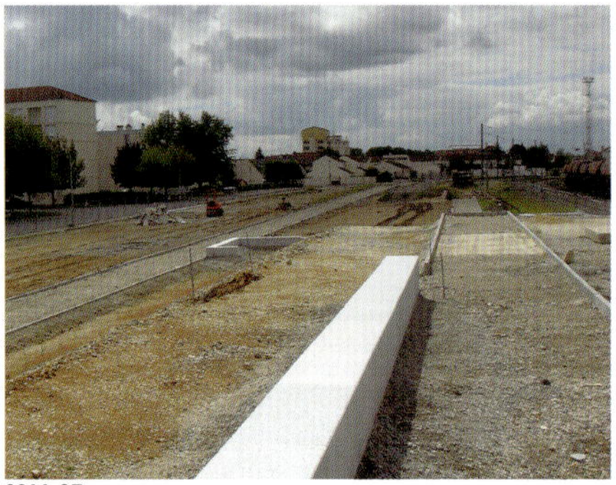
2011-07

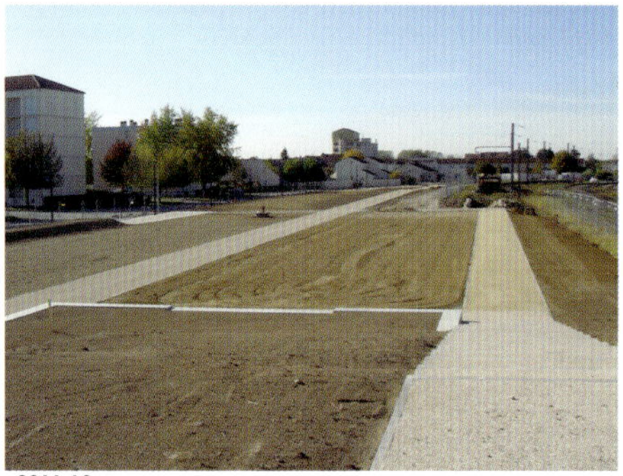
2011-10

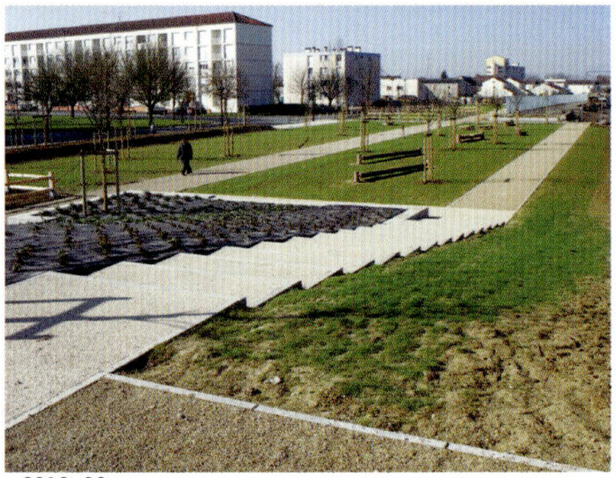
2012 -03

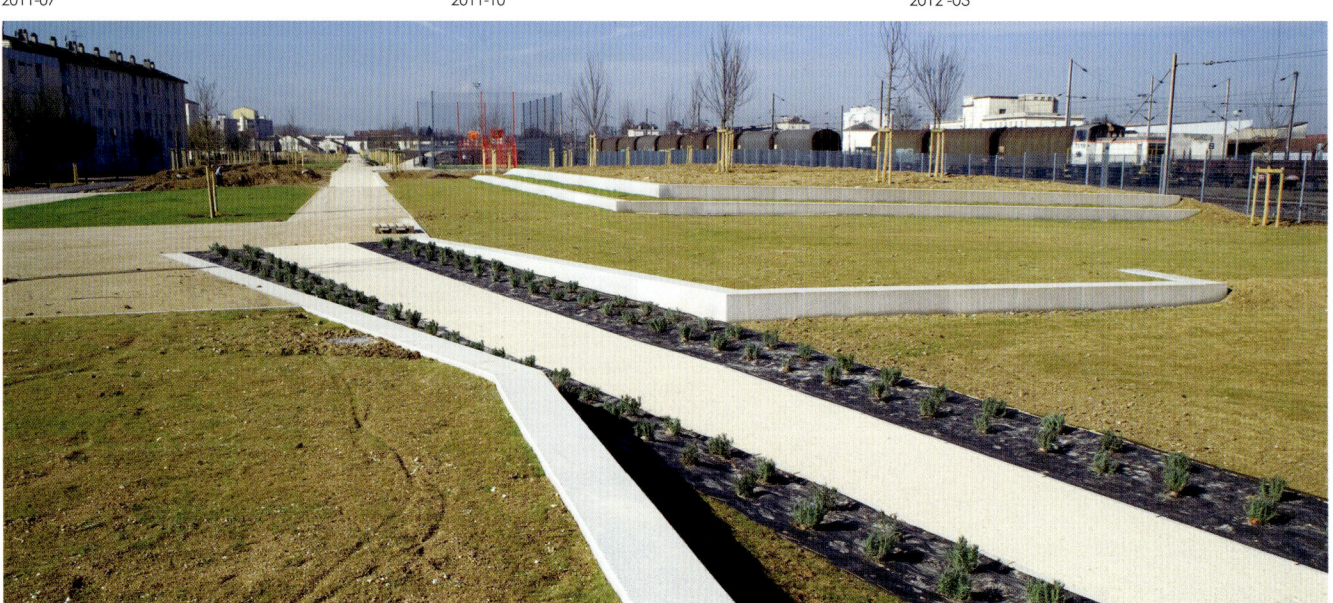

Opposite page: Transformation of the site and "construction" of the project over several months.
Above: The central lawn.

68

The station square, redeveloped as a new articulation point between the neighbourhood and the town centre for the arrival of the high-speed train line.

Croix de Metz neighbourhood

The whole of the Croix de Metz neighbourhood has been the subject of an urban renewal project since 2006. The demolition of horizontal housing blocks allowed us to rethink the neighbourhood's public spaces and to strengthen its character as a "park neighbourhood" with law housing density and planted with large trees.

Leuques avenue allowed us to unify the east and west part of the neighbourhood, run through with small squares and lanes.

Each housing block has been readdressed and reorganised in order promote the readability of the different spaces: the threshold of the building, parking and garden. A network of footpaths has been placed inside the housing grid, encouraging the neighbourhood's residents to meet each other.

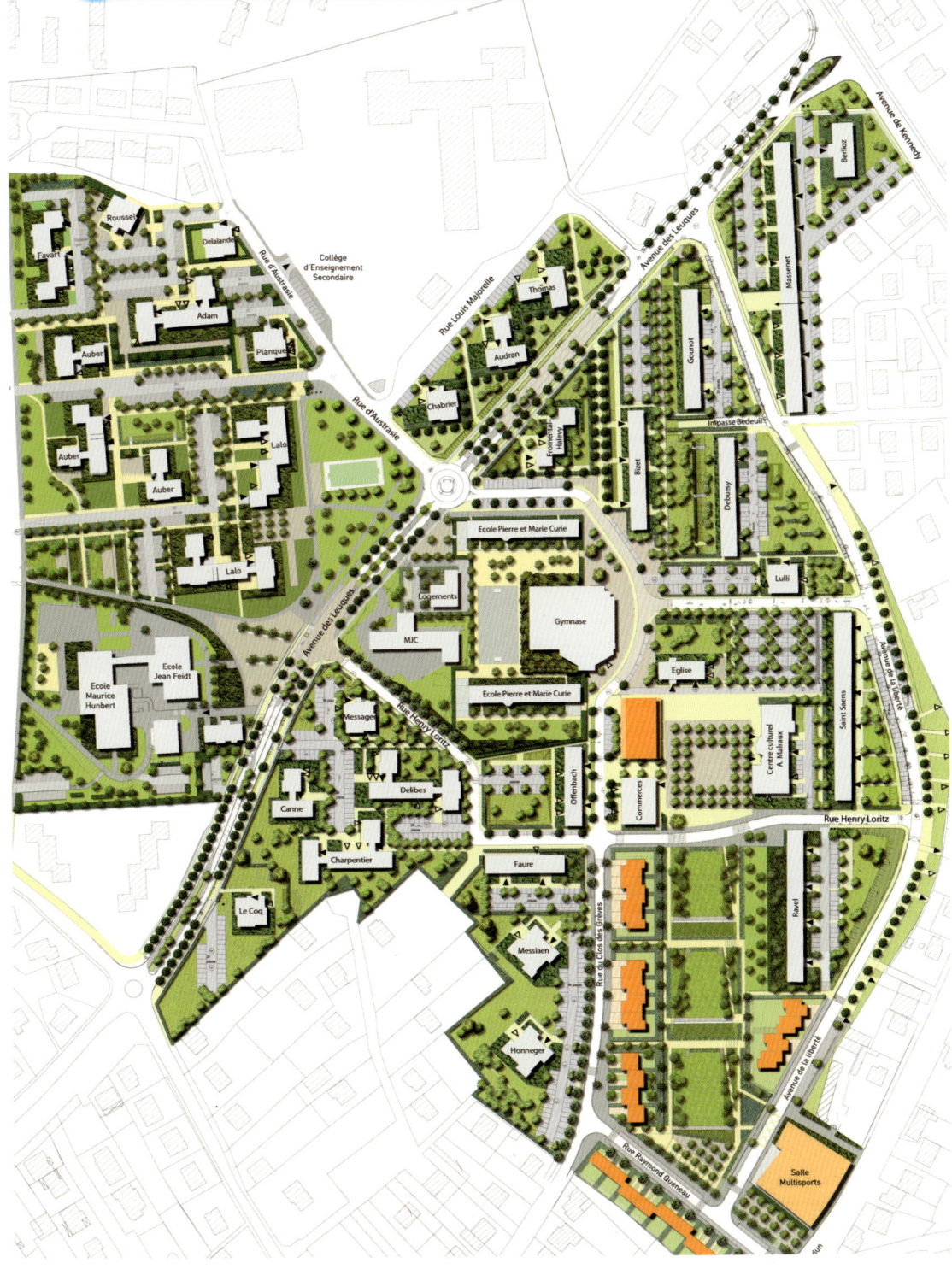

Opposite page: Before work began, an isolated and run-down neighbourhood.
Above: Site plan of the neighbourhood restructured by the landscape and rebuilding.

Above: Leuques avenue, a road transformed into a boulevard.
Opposite page: Jean Feidt square – the hillside landscape becomes part of the public space.

Opposite page: The apartment blocks and footpaths of a garden neighbourhood.
Above: The park before work began and during construction, revealing the relationship to the neighbourhood and the larger landscape.

the "naturbanity"

Concentrically or in patches, the city absorbs rural land. The countryside, which is always at the edges of cities, suffers from urban pressure. After a human exodus from the countryside to the city, it's the city that consumes the countryside. The lower price of land, and disenchantment with the city, makes the countryside more attractive. "Rurbanity" is a dominant system today which brings with it an over-consumption of agricultural space, a lack of facilities, and transport problems.

In our global society, thanks (or no thanks) to networks of all kinds, everything is becoming urban – even nature. The natural space itself attracts tourism and becomes an economic support. When it is over-used, natural space needs to be returned to nature and protected.

The honey from beehives in cities is better quality than the honey from the countryside. Organic agriculture seeks land in cities in order to develop a local market; meanwhile, pesticides pollute our countryside and our gardens.

The challenge of this nascent century is thus to bring the urban back to the cities, to limit urban spread, to preserve the countryside for non-polluting agriculture, and to restore natural space under the flag of preserving biodiversity. "Naturbanity" is the landscape equivalent of this urban movement.

The right to property was acquired during the French Revolution; a "right to the landscape" would allow a densification of the cities and an urban intensification, while structuring an environmental revolution.

After all the variants of garden cities, where the architectural form has determined the urban form, we are offering the idea of a landscape city where the void determines the solid.

Urban intensification via the landscape is our response to this problematic. The development of "nature in the city", the invention of new "natural urban parks" made up of community gardens and urban agriculture, and the structuring of new urban views through planting are among the solutions developed to circumscribe the city with the landscape.

Prés-Devant Park in Chalon-sur-Saône.

a "positive city"

Nature in the city is a recurrent request in urban projects, which must be given sense and content. Such a landscape risks being merely decorative if it is not designed to be sustainable. Vertical gardens or grassy tram platforms have attracted a lot of positive media coverage, but they are counterproductive in terms of sustainable development because they are great consumers of water.

Can the city positively generate environment in the same way that positive energy homes produce energy? To weave this positive city, we must work on enriching the warp and weft that compose it.

The mesh of viewpoints, from those that survey the landscape as a whole to those who think in terms of privacy, calls for a volumetric strategy of solids and voids that sculpt the space on scales that range from close proximity to that of the land area.

Green and blue grids, which can generate a diversity of environments and economy of water use, only work in a continuity that crosses the boundaries of land ownership and the operational perimeters.

The temporality of space forces us to think of the project in the long term by integrating the progression of its implementation, and a capacity for reversibility and adaptability. Taking the way it will be managed into account guarantees a sustainable project with the genes useful for its own evolution written into it.

The weave of boundaries and the precise noting of its degrees of porosity frame our practices. They ensure a reassuring sense of address situated in the city.

The sedimentation of historical traces and geographical layers in the making of a city strengthens the identity-forming references that avoid rootless collages.

We superimpose these urban layers in a reasoned and localised way, based on an order of priority, to design this positive city, this eco-neighbourhood project that we call a "landscape-city".

Seine hillsides

The French have been confronted with en epidemic of poor housing. All the town planning documents for the government's Grand Paris (Greater Paris) initiative talk of the necessity of building housing in the Ile de France region. The land available on the Andrésy hillsides, already served by public transport, represents an opportunity for urban development, but is also confronted with the apparently contradictory need to preserve the environment.

The landscape, made up of ecology and geography, of iconic views and the attachment of identity, of agricultural activity and subsistence gardening, is described in detail in order for it to become a structuring, newly valued and intangible element of the urban project.

The protection of two thirds of the wild and agricultural land through the creation of a Conglomeration Natural Park structures the town planning. It slides in between the plots of nearby organic agriculture, places ecological corridors between the river and the forest, develops the hedgerow vegetation structuring the borders and weaves in pathways to meet public transport, while a system of architecture in terraces opens up the views.

The transformation of a road into a boulevard on which a tramway runs will facilitate the creation of a new town centre linked to the Seine-side quays of the old centre. This new urban economy is a preservation strategy for a sustainable landscape that offers an escape from the problems of land falling into neglect and a shortage of housing.

- What will be the relationship between the valley and the hillsides?
A network of walks and landscape structures will link the Seine to Hautil via the hillsides.

81

- What will be the relationship between the town and the natural space?
The Andrésy hillsides will become a large inhabited park in a cultivated landscape (vegetable plots, peri-urban agriculture…).

- What will be the urban density and intensity?
Blocks with high density to preserve the landscape.

1	Le bois de l'Hautil / *The Hautil wood*
2	Le corridor écologique / *The ecological corridor*
3	Le parc des belvédères / *The "belvederes" park*
4	La ZAC des belvédères / *The "belvederes" ZAC*
5	Le cimetière / *The cemetery*
6	La mairie / *The town hall*
7	L'île Nancy / *Nancy island*
8	La RD 55 / *The RD55 road*
9	La gare / *The station*
10	L'ancien collège / *The old high school*

- What access to public transport will the neighbourhood have?
A network of pathways that lead to the station.

Mount Évrin park

Situated on old agricultural land, Mount Évrin park (around 20 hectares) forms the backbone of a new neighbourhood yet to be built. Stretching over 1.8km, the park provides a link between the old town, on a hillside in the Marne department, and the infrastructure and services of the new town of Marne-la-Vallée developed on the plateau.

Its atmosphere draws on the rural landscapes of the surrounding countryside: meadows, hedgerows, small woods and a broad wetland that came with the creation of a storm basin. At the heart of the housing, the Grand Orchard offers the most garden-like atmosphere in the park.

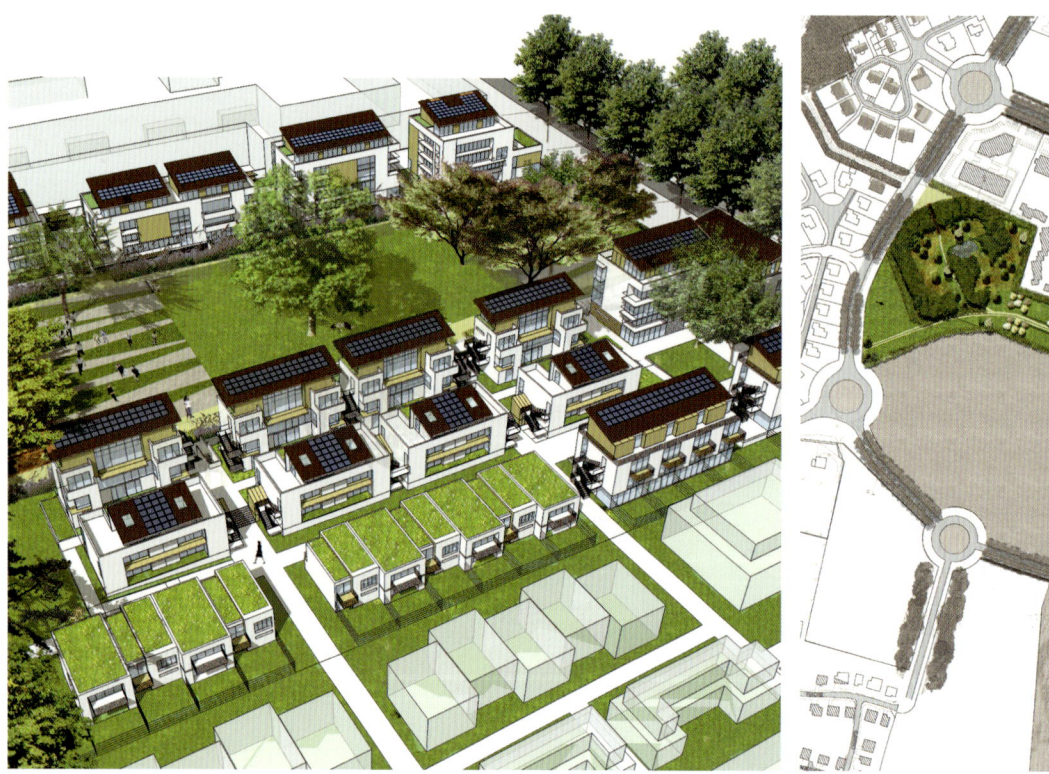

Enclosures allow for the cultivation of fruit trees, redcurrant bushes and hazel trees, whose fruit can be freely gathered by walkers. Elsewhere, meadows planted with standard fruit trees follow on from a sector of broom heath, then give way to a young woodland plantation.

Maturing into a natural space, the park evolves according to adapted management. It forms part of a deliberate approach to protecting and enhancing biodiversity through economical management. Only the edges of the paths are mowed regularly; the maintenance of the meadows is adapted to the flowering seasons and its use by the public. The hedges and drainage ditches are designed as ecological corridors, planted with hardy local species.

A similar dynamic has been developed in the planning of the eco-neighbourhood beside it: the landscape encroaches on the private lots. It allows for the organisation of different uses, and to ensure urban and ecological continuity between public and private spaces.

Opposite page: Axonometric diagram of a park block.
Above: Ground plan of the park structuring the eco-neighbourhood.

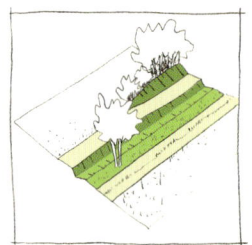

Above: Landscapes of the Brie plateau and the Marne hillsides, the vocabulary of the urban park.
Opposite page: The large meadow in July 2011.

Opposite page: Vocabulary and materials.
Above: The orchard – first act in the implementation of differentiated management.

Above: The large meadow in July 2011, showing its haymaking strategy.
Opposite page: A path through the orchard. Water collection underlies the park's organisation.

Haie Cerlin eco-neighbourhood

Situated in Seichamps, the sites for this project form one of the last reserves of unbuilt land in the greater Nancy area, and have been approached in terms of densification and the intensity of the landscape.

The 400 homes – facing south to maximise economy of energy and placed perpendicular to the slope to collect stormwater on the surface and allow it to percolate back into the ground – are organised around greens. These greens, places for neighbours to meet and use, are designed as shared spaces where the new "eco-practices" of the town will develop. Their landscape architecture is an environmental reinterpretation of the traditional farm layout in the villages of Lorraine.

Statements of Works define the environmental ambitions of the project in terms of architecture, town planning and landscape architecture. However, the planting of the boundaries between public and private space is already done when the plots are handed over to the construction firms in order to guarantee the future of the landscape structure.

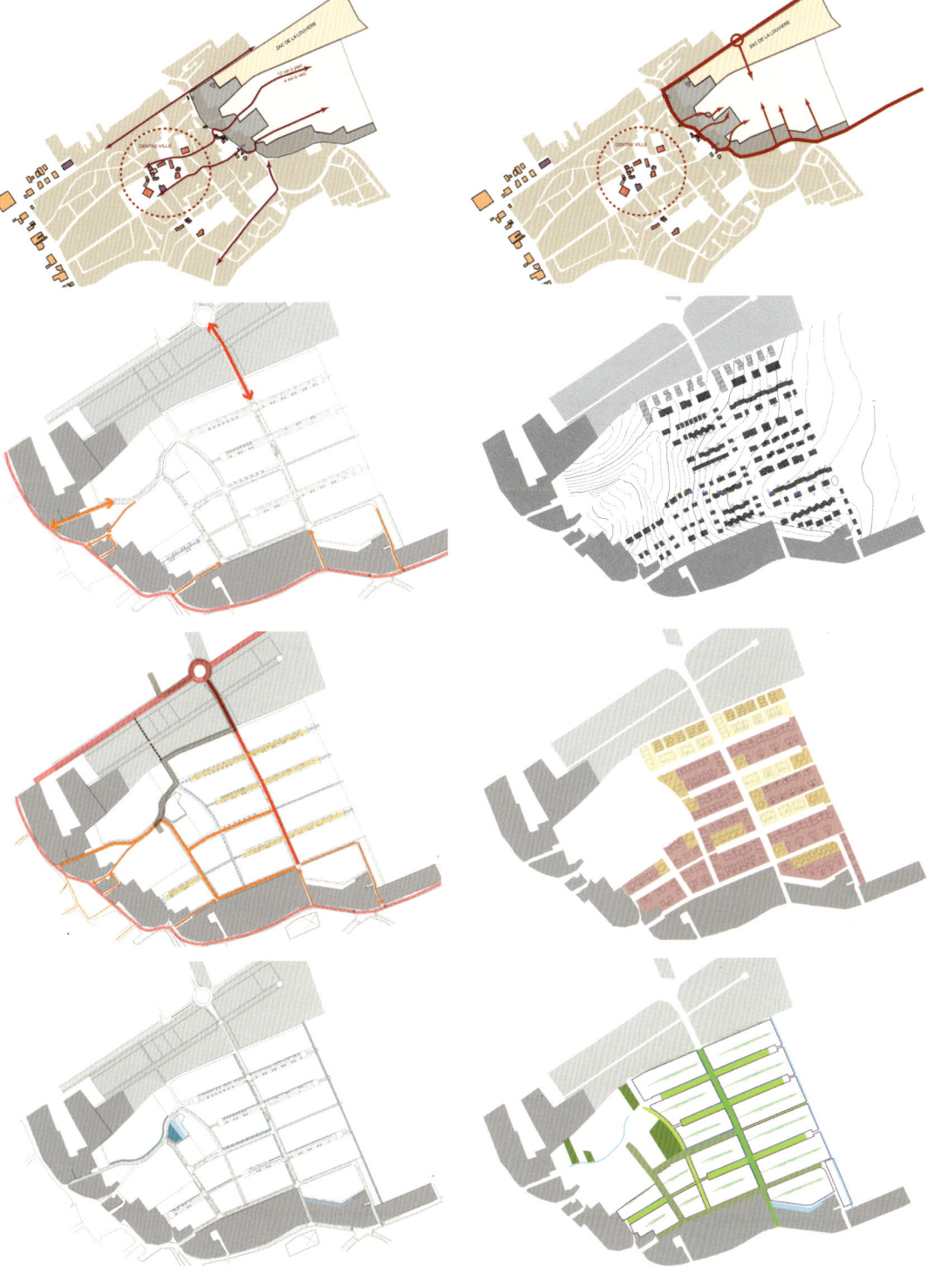

Opposite page: The location and boundaries of the eco-neighbourhood.
Above: Urban insertion and the planning grid, a way of considering urban, environmental and landscape continuity.

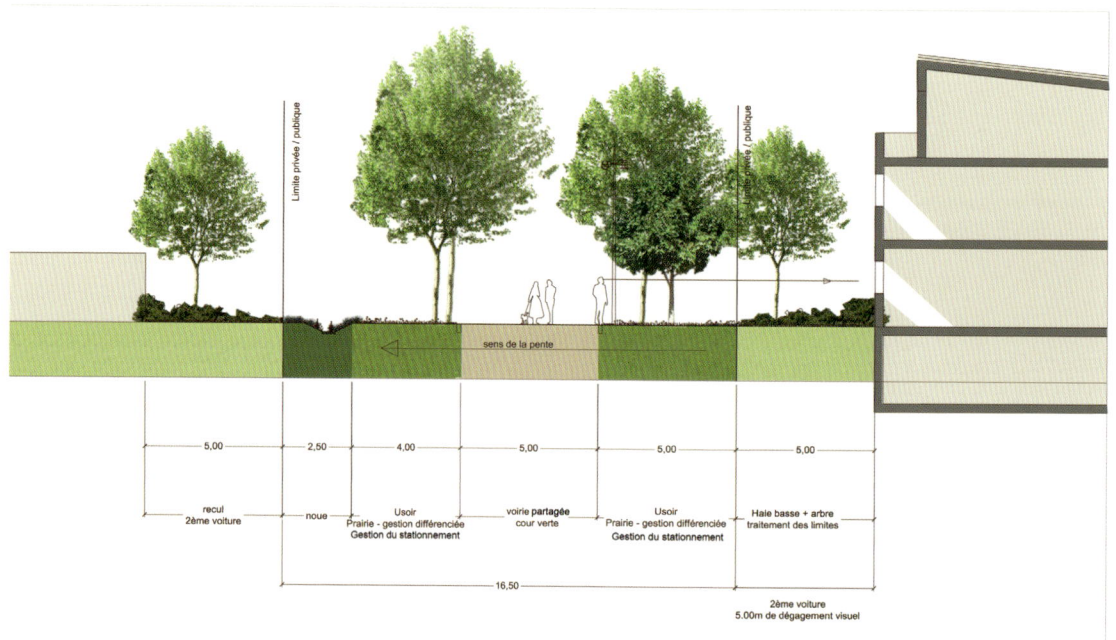

Above: Cross-section and artist's impression of a green, showing the contemporary interpretation of the "usoir" (front yards open to the road in Lorraine villages).
Opposite page: Suggested planting for the hedges on the private plots. General development plan, showing how the town planning is based on the detail of planting.

Principe de plantation des haies

Principe / distance plantation

Haie libre

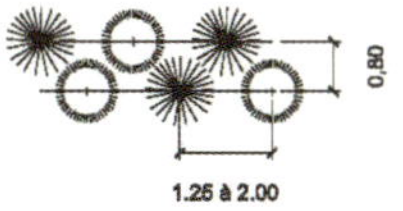

Haie taillée

Principe de plantation d'une haie double, multistrate

La multiplicité des troncs en cépée donne aux espaces plantés une forme de bosquet plus naturelle que celle des arbres tiges

Haie libre

Haie libre de composition symétriques semi persisitantes

Haie libre de composition symétriques semi persisitantes

Haie libre de composition symétriques semi persisitantes

Haie libre de composition asymétrique: grands arbustes au fond et petits arbustes devant

Haie taillée

Haie taillée entièrement caduque

Haie taillée 50/50 persistant/caduc

Haie taillée 50/50 persistant/caduc

Haie taillée 2/5 caduque 3/5 persistante

Haie taillée 1/3 caduque 2/3 persistante

93

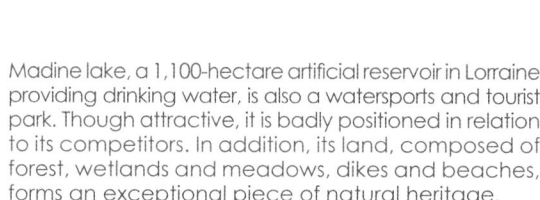

Madine lake

Madine lake, a 1,100-hectare artificial reservoir in Lorraine providing drinking water, is also a watersports and tourist park. Though attractive, it is badly positioned in relation to its competitors. In addition, its land, composed of forest, wetlands and meadows, dikes and beaches, forms an exceptional piece of natural heritage.

The economy of the site has to be reinvigorated with nature tourism that is less seasonal, and more consistent economic activity. The guide plan drawn up allows for the addition of new leisure facilities, a larger marina, accommodation and diversified leisure activities, while bringing out the specific qualities of the landscape.

The project is embedded in the environment and structures the natural leisure activities.

A "walkway building" – an 800-metre-long deck that forms a design line in the landscape – brings together the facilities, forms the gateway and the central feature of the site, is a launching point for walks, frames the views, shows where the urban ends and nature begins, and gives a radical new image to the site.

The architectural project for the site becomes a land-use project for the whole park.

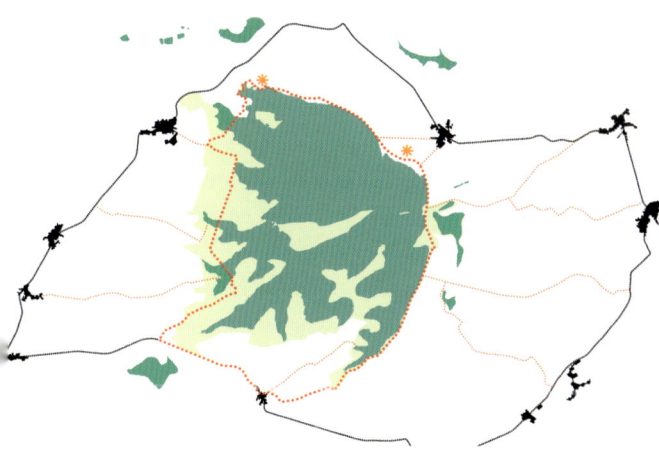
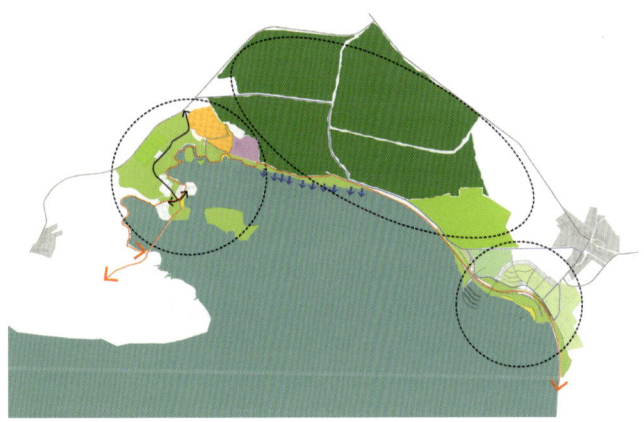

Opposite page: The site today as the motivation for the project.
Above: The project as a fusion of a site and its future uses.

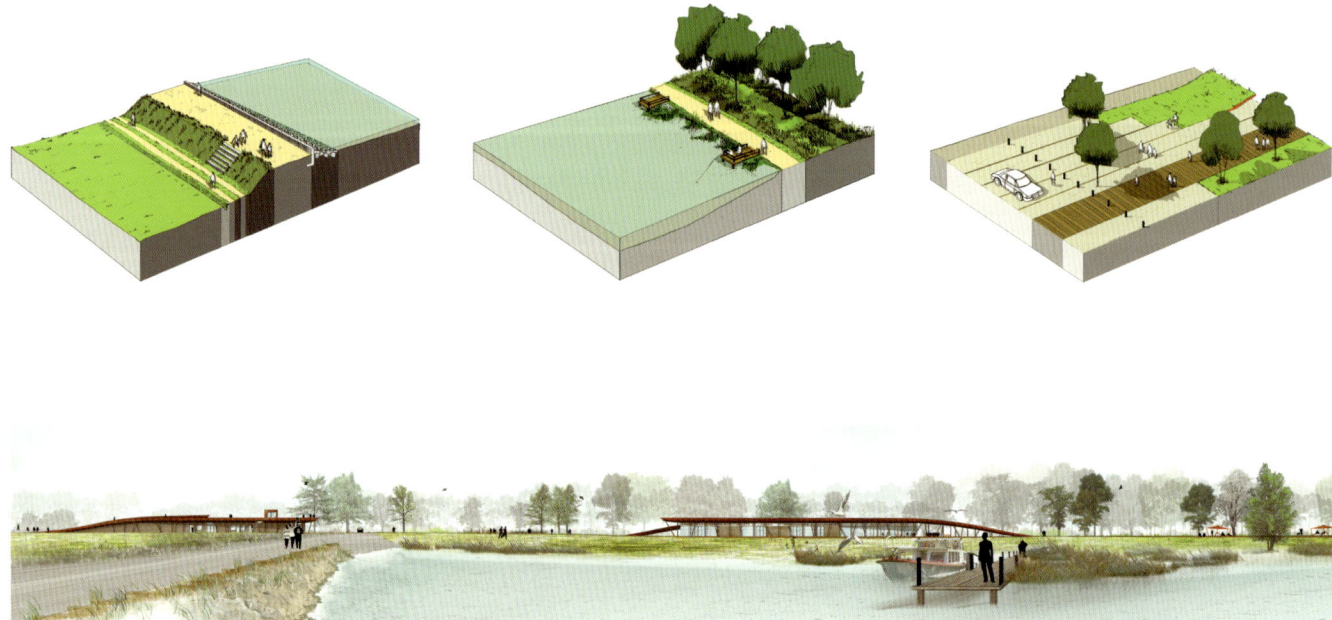

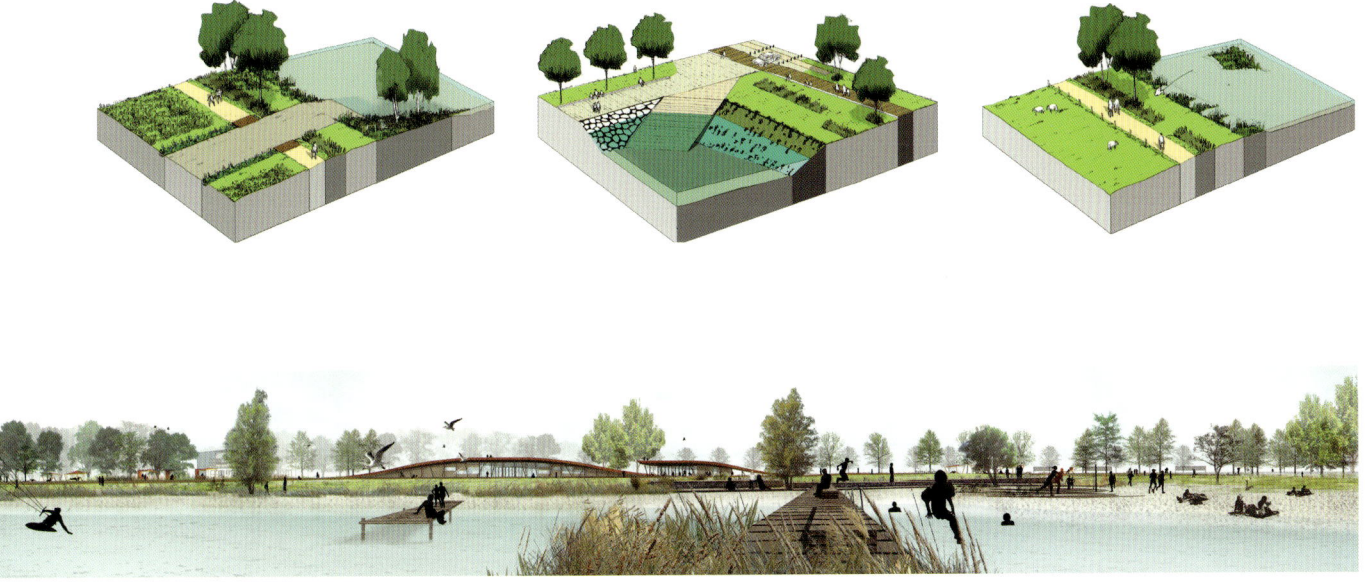

A walk that is open to the lakeside landscape and integrates the buildings.

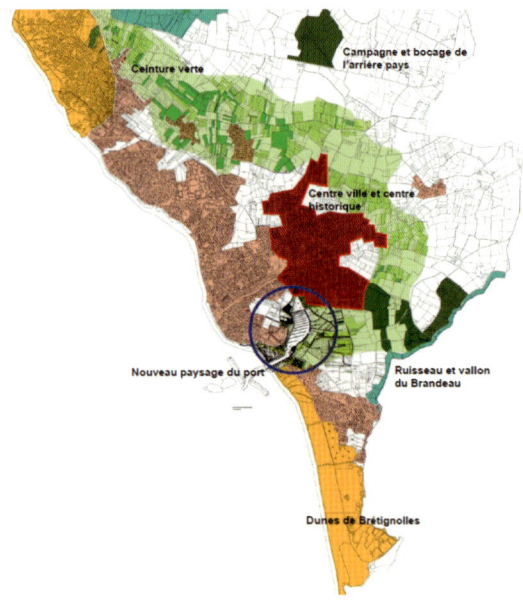 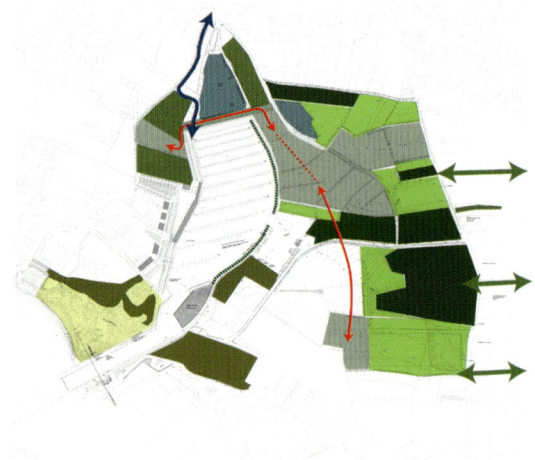

yachting marina

Situated on the Vendée coast and popular with tourists, Brétignolles-sur-mer is betting on halting suburban sprawl and creating a yachting marina to develop a new local economy. It has put in place a "green belt" to limit the spread of urbanisation; building plots will be transformed into woods and a port project is being developed.

The 10-hectare body of water created will provide mooring for 1,300 yachts. A quarry was reopened on the site to provide the riprap necessary to build the structures, before being backfilled by the earthworks generated by the basin.

The port project is ambitious from an environmental point of view, and seeks to minimise its impact on the natural spaces (minimal channel width, the use of riprap, parking on permeable ground, reusing the quarry, etc.).

A waterfront that prolongs the town is planned around the future port. The spaces around the basin are inspired by the landscapes of the site and perpetuate them: the dunes are returned to nature, the small fields and hedges and the wet meadows are protected and several hectares of young woodland have been planted.

Opposite page: The wooded green belt that halts urbanisation in order to create a new port economy.
Above: Ground plan of the port structure.

100

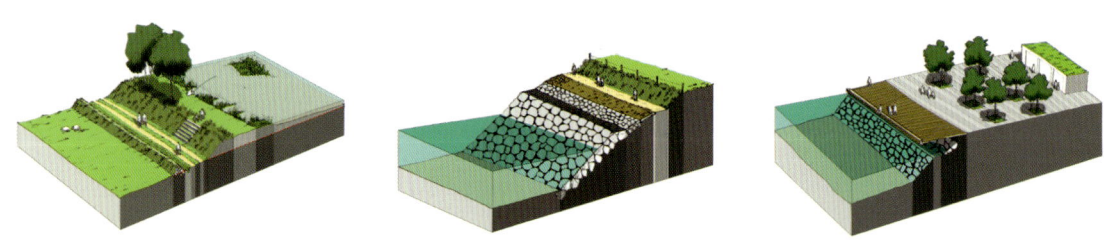

Opposite page: Management of the dredged waste and the backfill.
Above: The marina offers the opportunity to reconstruct natural environments and to rehabilitate the landscape.

102

Opposite page: The town quay and the channel.
Above: The marina from the land side and the bathing beach.

Limay port

The river port of Limay, on the Seine, is a multifunctional zone hosting commercial activities and heavy industry. In 2005, following on from the work of Patrick Colombier (the port's consultant architect between 2000 and 2004), a land-use and sustainable development plan was drawn up by the Ports of Paris. It was to become the port's guide plan in terms of strategies for economic development, enhancement and environmental protection, land-use planning and the occupancy of the area.

The challenge of this development strategy is to drive the development of river traffic by showing that the port activity can fit into its territory in a positive way, generating a beneficial landscape and a quality environment.

The development plan is both a strategic plan, a plan of action over several years, a means of managing the arrival of new businesses building their facilities on the site, and a town-planning and landscape document.

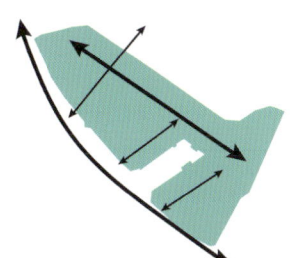
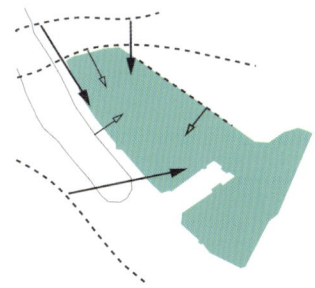

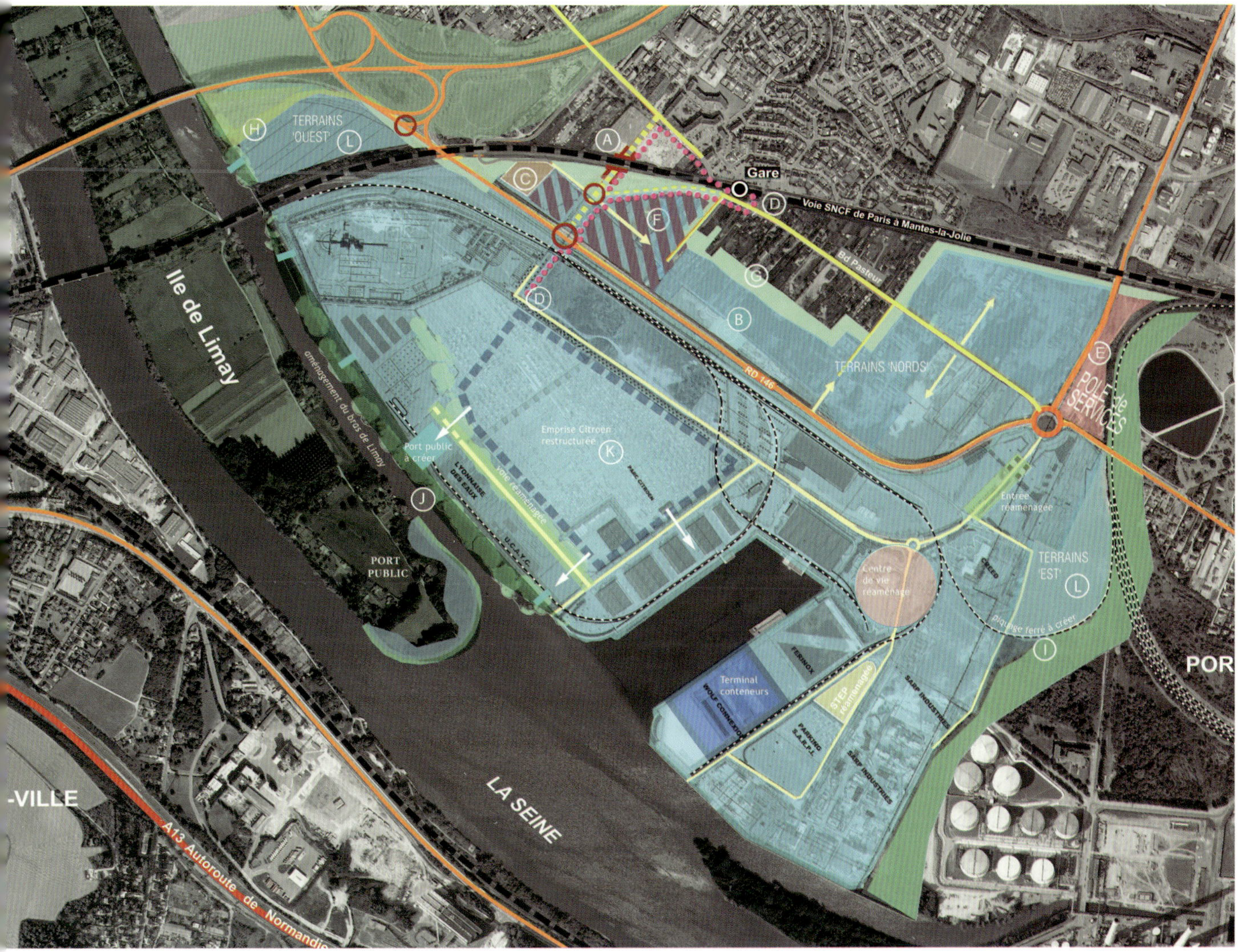

Opposite page: The views of the port, both distant and in proximity had to be maintained and strengthened – the Seine in Greater Paris exemplifies the confrontation of the city and nature.
Above: The Land-Use and Sustainable Development Plan for the Port of Limay, a guide plan for the city, the landscape and the environment.

To these ends, several documents were prepared: a plan for land development, a guide plan for the public spaces, a management plan for the green and natural spaces, a plan for planting and restoring denatured sites, and a Statement of Works covering urban, architectural, environmental and landscape specifications. "Green plans" programme the planting campaigns year on year and class in order of priority and frequency the maintenance of the different spaces. An agriculture style of management is favoured in order to minimise the costs of upkeep.

As land is acquired, broad parcels are integrated into the management plan. They are then sown, planted, maintained and become identifiable as belonging to the port. Progressively, the landscape of the port is constructed: industrial infrastructure is cheek by jowl with wide hay meadows, framed by hedgerows.

The architectural specifications include, among other things, a colour chart to guide the choice of colours on the buildings and smaller structures of the port. A range of bright and lively colours puts into relief certain architectural elements characteristic of port activity (silos, containers, chimneys, etc.).

Under the aegis of a nine-year town-planning and landscape mission, new buildings and operations have arrived, a controlled industrial landscape has taken shape, the structure has gained coherence and the environment blossomed. The permanent impact of these strategies makes the port of Limay a model for sustainable development.

Prés-Devant Park in Chalon-sur-Saône.

a new economy of landscape

Natural or human (!?) risks, induced by a predatory economy, are becoming more and more prevalent as the themes of landscape projects.

Rivers flood because their beds have been reduced by urban pressure and no longer absorb the excess water from the all-too-common land sealing. Alternative water management has become commonplace in urban projects, and forms the basis for a new development vocabulary.

Urban biodiversity has more chance of being regenerated than that of our countryside, which is pulverised by phytosanitary products. Differentiated management of the green spaces, decreasing the pressure of upkeep, is implemented together with an educational message about "weeds" in order to combat the frequently encountered lack of understanding on the part of the inhabitants.

Rivers that have become sterile conduits are the subjects for a reconquest of biodiversity space by giving riverbeds back their meanders and by restoring the banks through the soft technologies of civil engineering. We also design stormwater drainage works as river projects.

As the city moves forward, we discover discharges that are impossible to reabsorb. Gardens then become opportune for confining this irreversible pollution under a plant layer.

Over-visited natural sites are their own worst enemy. Tourist flow management and restoring these sites to nature are new applied sciences used by the landscape architect. Port projects, so necessary to the transport and leisure economy, need to be landscape projects to have a chance of reaching fruition.

The economy is perceived as a risk, but the benefits brought about by the economic development project can in part be directed upstream, to balancing out environmental and social factors and laying a better ground for its integration and acceptance in the landscape.

Hourdel point

Hourdel Point closes the southern part of the bay of the Somme. Its exceptional landscapes attract large numbers of visitors each year at high season. This intensive tourism is gradually deteriorating the natural environments of the point, which rely on a subtle balance between the dunes and the mud flats.

The decision to become designated as a "major site" necessitates finding a synergy between an attractive local economy, preserving of the value of the natural coastal environments and reconciling the district with the numbers of visitors it attracts. The natural site must be removed from the public in order to restore and protect it. This distance encourages respect for the area frequented by visitors and a channelling of tourist activities.

A well thought-out, large-scale plan for the management of traffic flow and parking is proposed, together with an upgrading of the hamlet of Hourdel and the natural space that surrounds it. The traffic strategy was planned taking into account the periods of high and low tourist attendance. With it comes a parking strategy that respects the use of the hamlet.

Footpaths link the parking areas to the larger landscape. They encourage a slow and progressive discovery of the site, invite visitors to dream and to approach the area with sensitivity.

Hourdel Point: How to reconcile tourist pressure and the preservation of natural spaces.

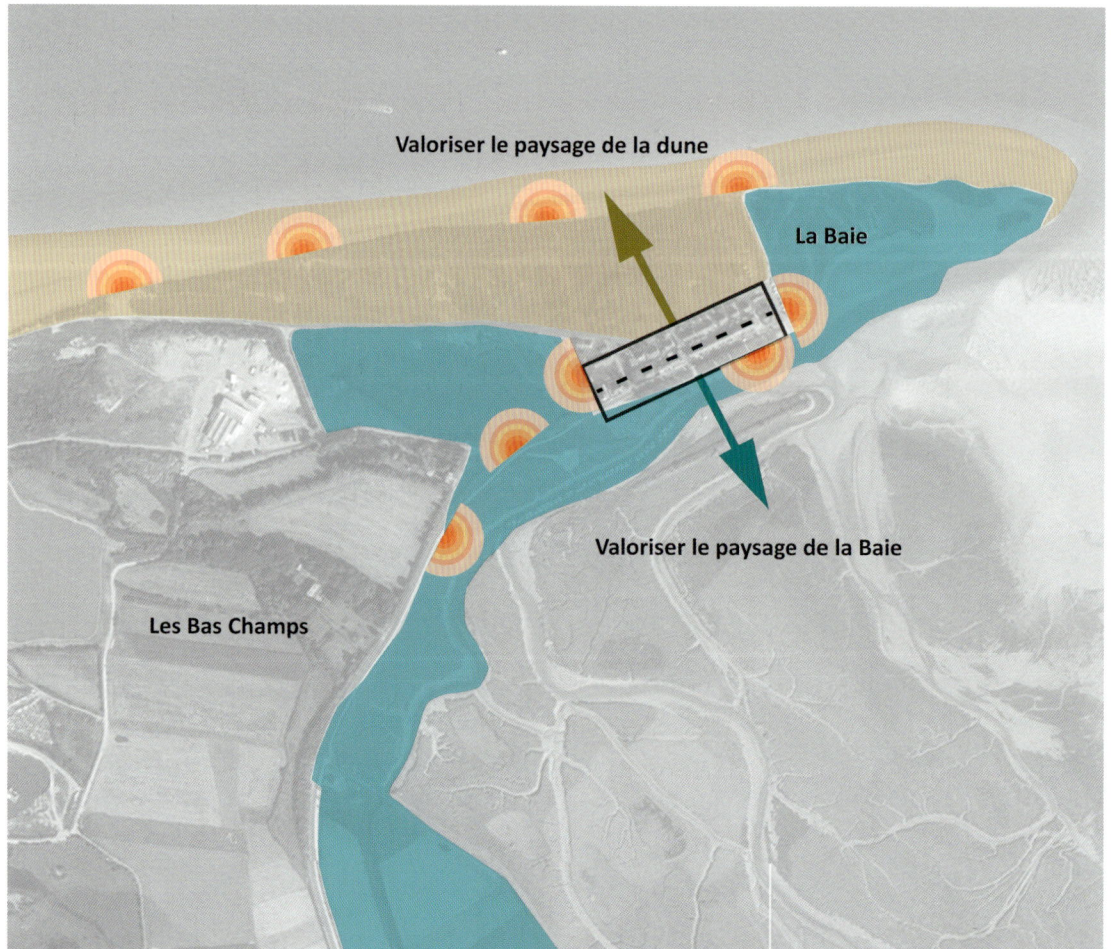

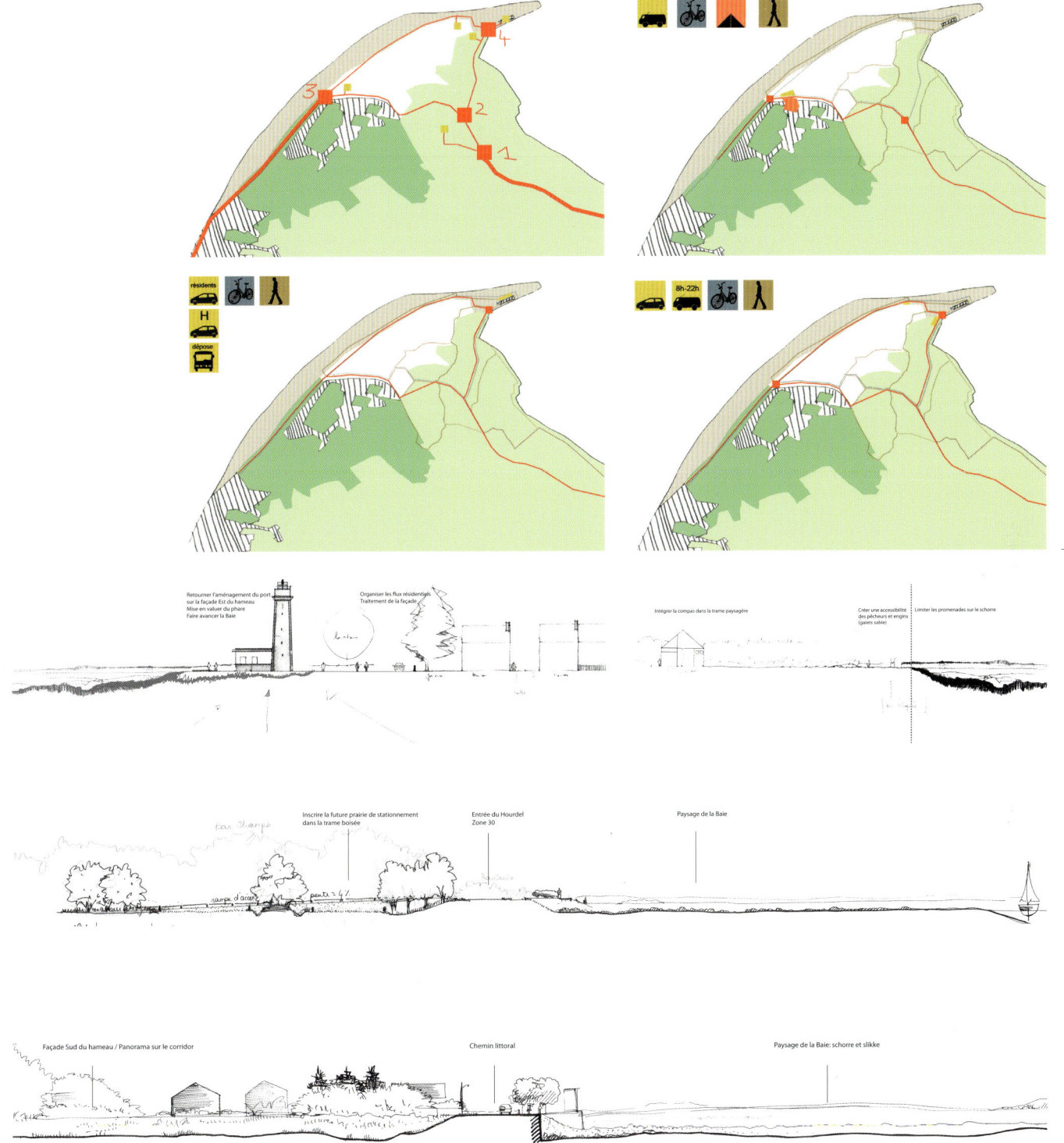

Opposite page: Strategic plans for the management of the flow of tourists and making the most of the natural spaces.
Above: Development sequences.

Saint-Laurent River

Situated in a valley with steep escarpments, the hamlet of Gournay is regularly flooded by the Saint-Laurent River culvert, by its abandoned industrial reach, and by the discharge from high plateaux that have lost their permeability. A competition launched in 2004 called for bids to resolve the flooding problems by creating a new river bed at the lowest point of the valley.

This hydraulic project, which calls for a restructuring of the area, is thus both an urban and an environmental project. Along the river's route public spaces and traffic circulation has to be reorganised, land lots regrouped, public facilities rebuilt and houses destroyed or relocated.

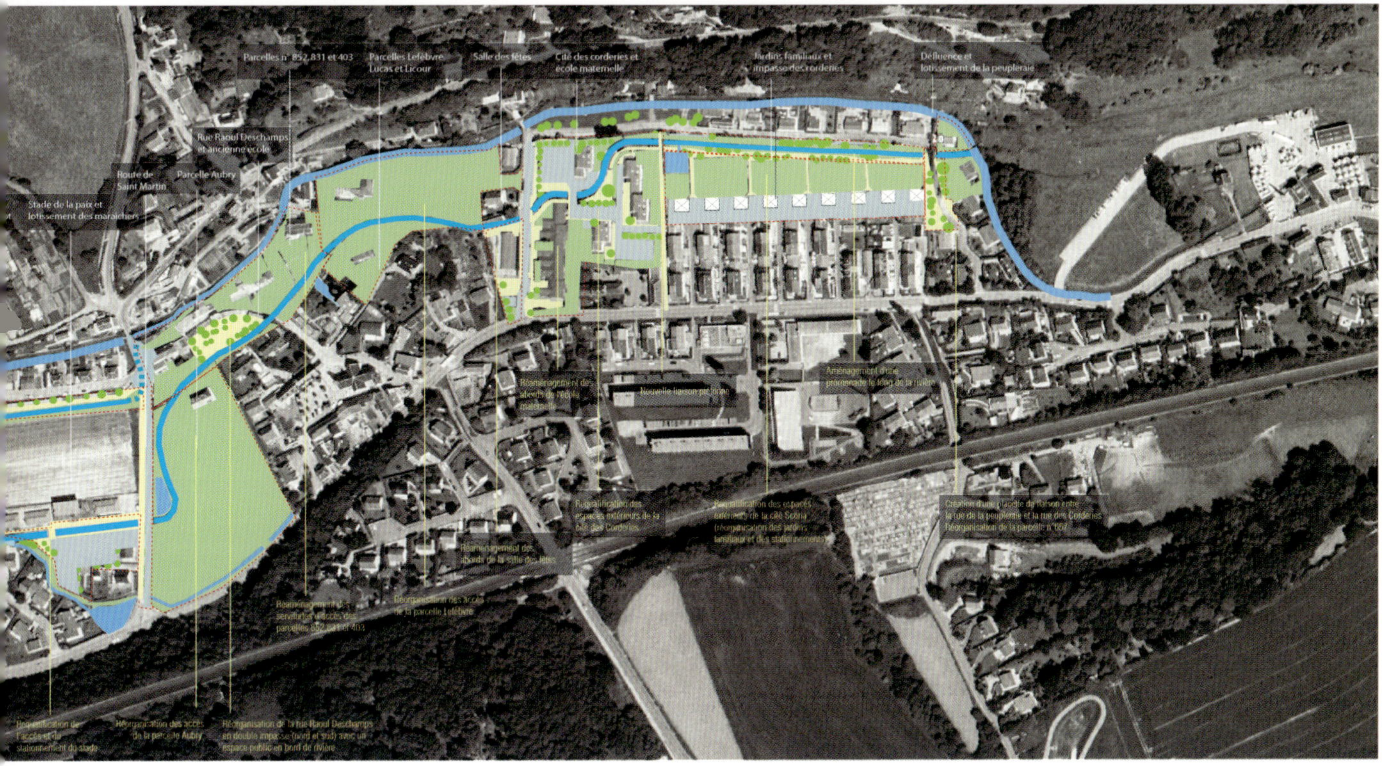

117

The hamlet of Gournay, the course of the Saint-Laurent and its reach. Combatting flooding becomes an incentive for urban restructuring.

Zone d'inondation potentielle au
passage des eaux de débordement
du Saint-Laurent
Zone de ruissellement préférentiel
HAUTEUR D'EAU (m)

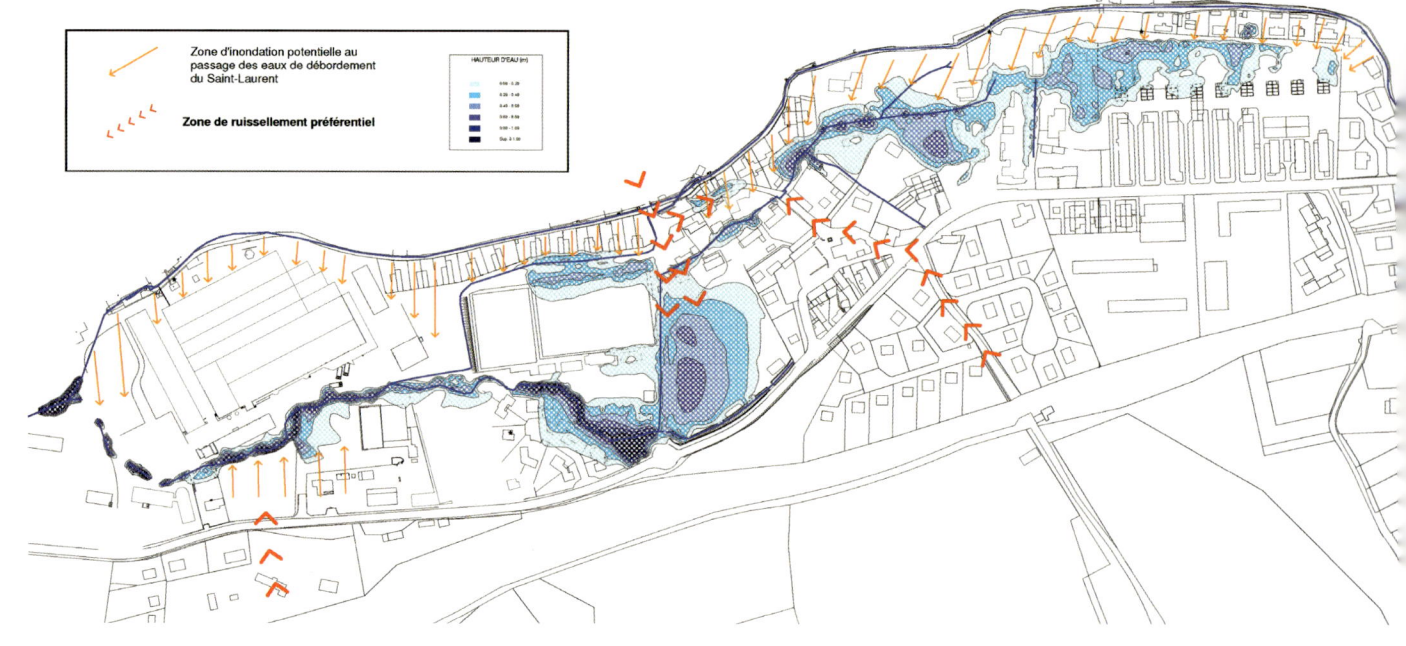

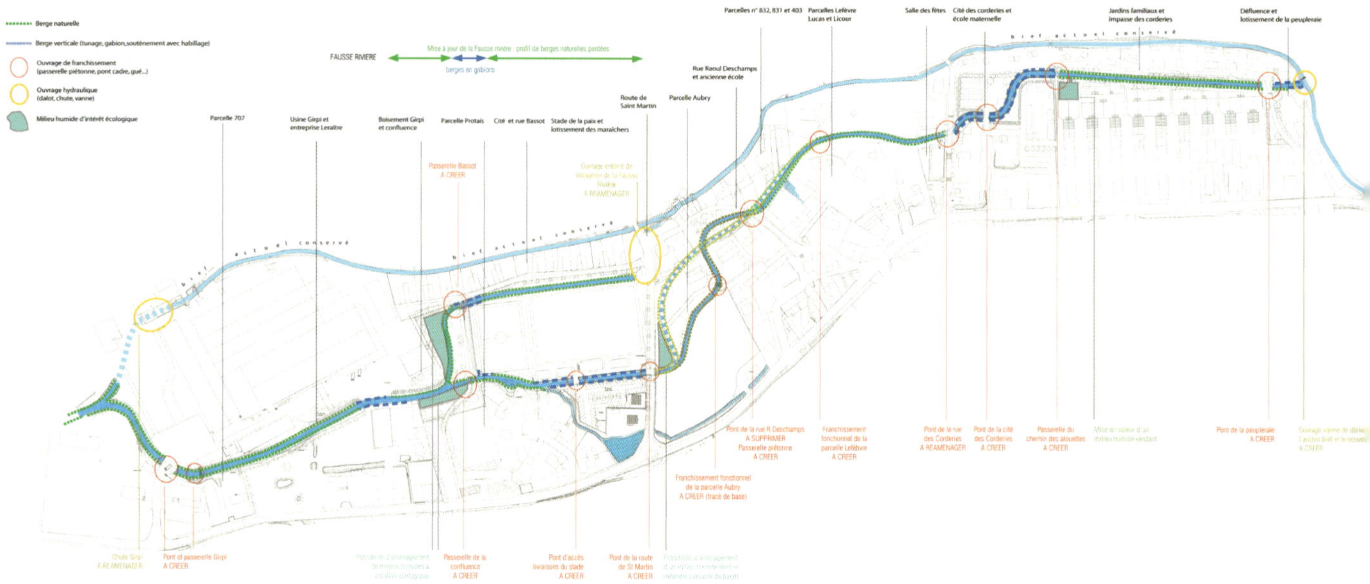
Berge naturelle
Berge verticale (tunage, gabion, soutènement avec habillage)
Ouvrage de franchissement
(passerelle piétonne, pont cadre, gué...)
Ouvrage hydraulique
(dalot, chute, vanne)
Milieu humide d'intérêt écologique
FAUSSE RIVIERE
Mise à jour de la Fausse rivière : profil de berges naturelles pentées
berges en gabions
Parcelle 707
Usine Girpi et
entreprise Leraître
Boisement Girpi
et confluence
Parcelle Protais
Cité et rue Bassot
Stade de la paix et
lotissement des maraîchers
Route de
Saint Martin
Parcelle Aubry
Rue Raoul Deschamps
et ancienne école
Parcelles n° 832, 831 et 403
Parcelles Lefèvre
Lucas et Licour
Salle des fêtes
Cité des corderies et
école maternelle
Jardins familiaux et
impasse des corderies
Défluence et
lotissement de la peupleraie
bief actuel conservé
Passerelle Bassot
A CREER
Ouvrage enterré de
Rivière
A REAMENAGER
Chute Girpi
A REAMENAGER
Pont et passerelle Girpi
A CREER
Passerelle de la
confluence
A CREER
Pont d'accès
livraisons du stade
A CREER
Pont de la route
de St Martin
A CREER
Franchissement fonctionnel
de la parcelle Aubry
A CREER (tracé de base)
Pont de la rue R.Deschamps
A SUPPRIMER
Passerelle piétonne
A CREER
Franchissement
fonctionnel de la
parcelle Lefèbvre
A CREER
Pont de la rue
des Corderies
A REAMENAGER
Pont de la cité
des Corderies
A CREER
Passerelle du
chemin des alouettes
A CREER
Pont de la peupleraie
A CREER

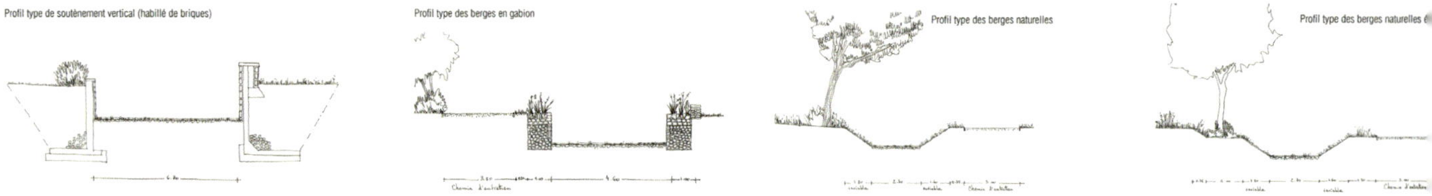
Profil type de soutènement vertical (habillé de briques)
Profil type des berges en gabion
Profil type des berges naturelles
Profil type des berges naturelles

Initially aimed at finding a zero risk solution, the hydraulic programme has evolved towards a reasonable management of the risks after studies found that total protection was not be possible. The project no longer combats flooding but aims to minimise its consequences. The community now buys back the floodable houses to rebuild them on stilts, and the river has been landscaped with a more natural profile that can evacuate the water rapidly. The water course is no longer an anti-flood construction, but a natural space that "manages" a natural risk.

Through a strong programme of consultation, with major investment by the local authorities, the population is closely involved with this environmental revolution and urban change. Slowly, the project has fitted into the reality of the area and society's evolution in relation to natural phenomena.

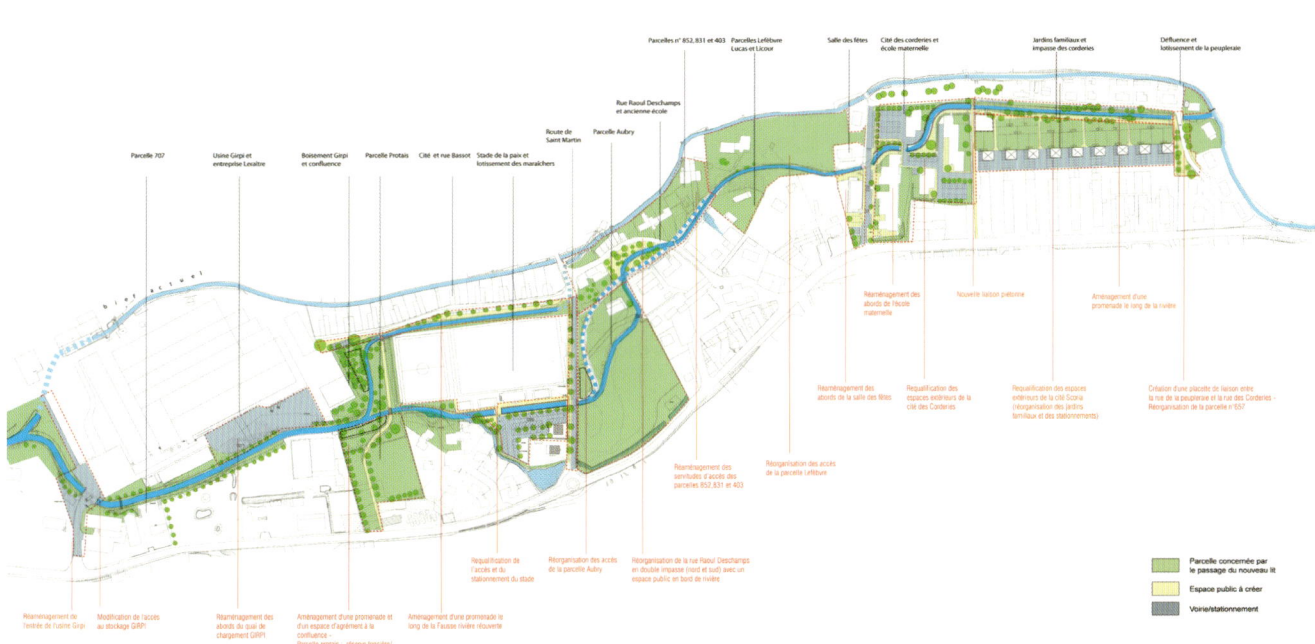

Opposite page: The 50-year floodmark, and the different bank typologies proposed.
Above: The different projects for public spaces brought about by the new river.

Prés-Devant suburb

The building of Chalon-sur-Saône's new hospital, together with the completion of the bypass, imposed a need for retroactive thinking about the whole suburb of Prés-Devant. On the table were: redefining the public spaces, traffic flow, the development of a medical cluster, reducing uncontrolled landfill, combatting invasive plants and flood management for the River Thalie, all within a very limited project budget.

The old departmental road becomes the main walk through the park; the containment of the landfill creates a new topography; the Thalie wetlands become gardens; and the public park is floodable. Taking the constraints and residual problems as the basis for a project generates a new landscape, normalised and positive.

Prés-Devant park fits into the agricultural landscape of the Thalie valley, allows for the expansion of the river under flood and gives the new hospital neighbourhood its identity.

Two stages of the site under construction.
Top: The Prés-Devant sector during its clean-up.
Above: The road becomes a walk through the park and the landfill a lake.

Above: The wetland landscape in the background.
Opposite page: The park, including during a winter flood.

123

Above: Before work began in 2008, and after completion. In the background is Chalon hospital (architects: Agence Brunet Saunier). Opposite page: The park, a natural urban space.

Gassets brook

Gassets brook, a stream running down from the Briard plateau, structures the town of Serris. The development programme envisaged lining the stream and channeling it underground to transform it into a wastewater facility beneath the public space.

The main challenge of the project was to convince the local authority to keep the stream above ground and to enhance it by the creation of connected public spaces. The project therefore suggests an alternative stormwater management system and transforms the banks into a floodable walk.

The significant gradient between the stream and the public invites a varied vocabulary of talus, willow fascines and gabions. Several sequences create a journey from the "natural" stream to its outfall into a large storm basin. The stream opens onto the town through a series of lookout points and holds sloping towards the water. Paths and flights of steps allow the public to go down to the brook and sit on its banks.

Riverside vegetation and wet meadows encourage a specific biodiversity, producing an effect of "nature in the town". Recently, however, over-intensive management of the vegetation has undercut the richness of the environment. This project proves to what point the question of management is vital. By drawing up a management plan it will be possible to follow and encourage its evolution over time.

The project generates a landscape and an environment born of the waterproofing of urban ground.

Opposite page: The lookout point over the storm basin.
Above: Steps down to the brook and details of the restructuring work. A wastewater project turned urban project.

projects index

 pp.014-019

 pp.020-025

 pp.026-029

 pp.030-035

 pp.036-039

 pp.040-045

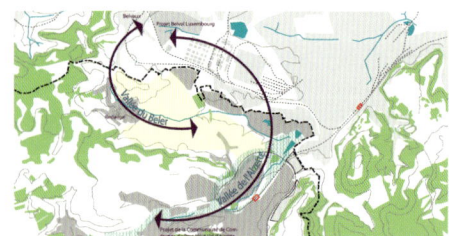 pp.046-051

 pp.052-055

 pp.058-063

pp.064-069

pp.070-075

pp.080-081

pp.082-089

pp.090-093

pp.094-097

pp.098-103

pp.104-111

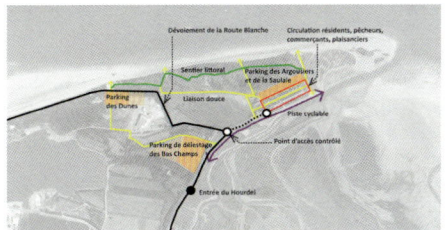
pp.112-115

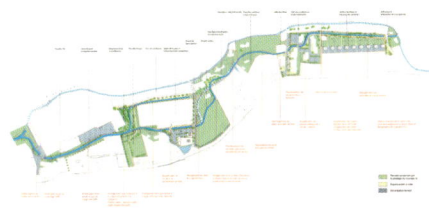
pp.116-119

pp.120-125

pp.126-129

biography-agency

Jean-Marc Gaulier (born in 1958) is a town-planner, landscape architect and chartered (DPLG) architect. He created the Urbicus agency in 1996, developing a practice that sees itself as an "architecture of the land", driven by landscape architects.

Between 1985 and 1995, at Alexandre Chemetoff's Bureau des Paysages (Office of Landscapes), he learnt by example and practiced the project, leading to his acceptance as a chartered landscape architect by the French Landscape Federation. In 1998 he began teaching at the National School of Higher Studies in Nature and Landscape Architecture in Blois (ENSNP), where he was successively co-director of the 4th year project course on "major landscapes", then of the 3rd year workshop on urban projects. In 2010, thanks to his experience as a landscape architect-town planner, he joined the National Agency for Urban Renewal (ANRU) centre of expertise.

Today, 16 years on and with 20 team members, Urbicus continues to structure itself to capitalise on its experience, and to increase its capacity to share it, and to claim, through practice, a more structuring role for landscape architects in land-use planning.

contributions

Currently working on Urbicus projects:

Tanja Aubourg, Claire Bellet, Rudy Blanc, Thomas Boisdet, Rostom Chikh, Olivier Courtelle, Amandine Doucet, Thimothé Dumas, Sandrine Feutry, Véronique Fourteau, Simon Gaulier, Sylvie Gourio, Évelyne Henriot, Noëlle Madrona, Bernadette Muchenberger, Solène Quilin, Chrystelle Rouge and Amina Zehouani.

Contributors to the projects presented in this book and other projects:

Johanna Almgred, Yuli Atanassov, Grégoire Bassinet, Clément Bollinger, Élodie Bortoli, Marc de Verneuil, Federica Dell'Orto, Antoine du Plessis d'Argentré, Bénédicte Dufieux, Agathe Gresset, Guillaume Hugon, Soizic Larpent, Gaylord Le Goaziou, Marielle Lévy, Yohann Maillard, Luc Mallet, Maud Martzolf, Bénédicte Morel, Florent Morisseau, Grégory Ouint, Nicolas Renard, Jérôme Saint Chély, Olivia Samit, Laurence Sciascia, Lionel Sikora, Rémy Turquin, Anne-Sophie Verriest.

This book was made possible by:

Sandrine Feutry and Chrystelle Rouge

Our thanks to everyone for their professionalism, their work and their motivation.

credits

Texts, images and photographs: © Urbicus

except

A3 Production – p.44 four photos at the top
Agence Com'Air – p.121
Print (private collection) – p.30 top left
Old postcards (private collection) – p.40 left
Jean-François Chapuis / Photothèque Smac – p.12, p.15 top
Éric Giretti – p.94
Ville de Gonfreville L'Orcher – p.117 top
Gras Miroux Architectes associés – p.82
Image in Air - p.101 top
François Marchand / Balloïde-photo – p.30 right, p.32-33 bottom
Éric Morency – p.27, p.126
Old photographs of Petite Rosselle (private collections) – p.53 top
Sogreah – p.118 top
Terre d'images – p.37

Part of the photographic images credited to Urbicus was taken by:
Charles Delcourt and Michel Reuss

The perspective drawings are by:
Cube
Jean Joyon
Gaël Morin
Chloé Sanson

Open-air theatre in Mantes-la-Jolie, 2006.

©2012 by Design Media Publishing Limited
This edition published in November 2012

Design Media Publishing Limited
20/F Manulife Tower
169 Electric Rd, North Point
Hong Kong
Tel: 00852-28672587
Fax: 00852-25050411
E-mail: Kevinchoy@designmediahk.com
www.designmediahk.com

Author: Jean-Marc GAULIER
Editing: ICI Interface (ICI Consultants), Paris, France
Chief Editor: Chia-Ling CHIEN
Assistant Editor: Nicolas BRIZAULT
English Translation: Alison CULLIFORD
Graphic Design: Wijane NOREE
Design/Layout: Karine de MAISON

Création de la collection «Green vision» et sa première
édition française (bilingue français-anglais)
© ICI Consultants, Paris, France, 2012
www.ici-consultants.com
contact@ici-consultants.com
Tel: +33 (0)1 48 87 08 15
Fax: +33 (0)1 42 01 01 27

All rights reserved. No part of this publication may be
reproduced or transmitted in any form or by any means,
electronic or mechanical, including photocopy, recording
or any information storage and retrieval system, without
prior permission in writing from the publisher.

ISBN 978-988-15661-7-1

Printed in China